Money Matters...

WHAT STOCKBROKERS DON'T ALWAYS TELL YOU....

by Richard DuPuis, CFP

MONEY MATTERS
What Stockbrokers Don't Always Tell You . . .
By Richard DuPuis, CFP
Copyright 1990 by Richard DuPuis
Produced by Wright & Ratzlaff Associates
Cover Design: Robert Wright
Published by Companion Books, Inc.
900 North Federal Highway, Suite 160-27
Boca Raton, FL 33432
All rights reserved. No part of this book may be reproduced, stored in a retrieval system, or transmitted, in any form or by any means, electronic, mechanical, photocopying, recording, or otherwise, without the written permission of the publisher.
Printed in the United States of America
ISBN: 0-9623830-0
Library of Congress No. 89-92118
Price: $12.95

This book is available at special rates for use in promotions, fund raisings or as a premium. This book also can be personalized for your use. Write Companion Books at 900 North Federal Highway, Suite 160 - 27, Boca Raton, FL 33432 or telephone 1-800-962-5564.

DEDICATION

This book is dedicated to professionals in all fields that really do put their client's interests first.

ACKNOWLEDGMENTS

Writing and publishing a book takes a lot of time and assistance from others. Naturally, it's difficult to cite everyone that has helped along the way, but I want to especially thank my wife, Gale, for her steadfast encouragement, and to both of our families, for providing the environment as we grew up, to help us believe we can achieve anything. And while it is hundreds of miles and a quarter of a century away, I will always be grateful to the *Sault Star* for giving me the opportunity to report. Thanks also, to my dedicated journalism instructors at the University of Florida. For his encouragement that there was a real need for a book like this, I thank Wayne Ezell. Pat Elich deserves a real big thank you for taking the time to edit down tons of writing to make it easier for you to read and Paul Matecki for making sure everything written was legal. Thanks also to Margo Wallace and Charlene Perrone, who helped with the cover design and layout. I would like to sincerely thank Betty Wright for her guidance throughout this undertaking. And put the spotlight on Martin Coyne, for he was the catalyst. His belief in my ideas has meant a lot to me.

CONTENTS

SECTION ONE:
PLANNING YOUR FINANCES 15

1. **JOINT OWNERSHIP** 17
   When Not to Use It 17
   Joint Tenancy Can Lead to Trouble 19
2. **YOUR WILL** 23
   Wills Before 1981 Could Have Major Faults 23
   Wills Don't Always Do What You Want 24
   Important Reasons for Revising Your Will 26
   Things to Consider Before Seeing the Attorney 28
3. **SAVING ON ESTATE TAXES** 32
   How to Get Up to a 90% Discount 32
   Flower Bonds Blossom at Death 34
4. **TRUSTS** 37
   Trusts for Second Marriages 37
   Trusts for Single People 39
   Placing Your Trust in a Trust 41
5. **ESTATE PLANNING STRATEGIES** 44
   Estate Planning for the Not So Rich 44
   Choosing the Right Evaluation Date 46
   Correct Planning for Insurance Benefits
      at Death 49
   Correct Use of Powers of Attorney 52
6. **FINANCIAL PLANNING** 55
   A Good Financial Plan is Your Key to Success 55
   What to Expect From a Good Planner 57
   What to Confide to Your Planner 60
   Some Things Should Not Be Put Off 62
   Simple Things a Planner Might Quickly Spot 64
   Financial Planning for the Young 66
   Wives Should Be Involved 68

7. CHARITABLE STRATEGIES   71
Advantages of Donating Stock for You
   and Charity   71
This Charitable Trust Doubles as a Tax Shelter   73
Charitable Trusts Help You and Loved Ones   75
Charitable Donations That Pay "You"
   at Income Tax Time   77

8. BUYING INSURANCE   80
Using Insurance to Bind Top Executives   80
Disability Can Threaten Your Future   82
Insurance You Use While You are Alive   84
How to Plan for Short Term Risks   87

9. RETIREMENT PLANNING   90
Can You Afford to Live on Golden Pond?   90
Figuring Out How Much You Will Need
   at Retirement   92
Your Options, if Your Plan is Canceled   94
Tax Reform Changes IRA Withdrawal Rules   97
Putting Your IRA Dollars to Work   99
Try this IRA Substitute for Saving   102

10. SPECIAL INSURANCE NEEDS   106
Nursing Home Care — Protect Yourself Now   106
Big Storms Can Require Special Insurance   108

SECTION TWO:
THE STOCK MARKET   111

11. BROKERS   113
Shopping Tips for Finding the Right Broker   113
How to Get Rid of Brokers' Annoying Calls   115

12. MEASURING THE ECONOMY   119
Your Keys to Measuring the Economy   119
How to Predict Interest Rate Directions   121

13. DIVERSIFICATION AND RISK   125
Asset Allocation Always Makes Sense   125
Diversification Safeguards Against Unknown   127
Define Your Definition of Risk   129
Sensible Diversification Ideas   131

14. USE OF MARGINS   134
Taking Advantage of Tax Deductible
   Margin Interest   134

Don't Let Margin Get Out of Control   137
How Margin Will Magnify Your Results   140
15. OPTIONS   143
Stock Insurance Fights Indigestion   143
16. MUTUAL FUNDS   146
When Your Mutual Fund Can Be Taxing   146
Why Hoppers Finish Last   148
17. BONDS   151
A Simple Formula to Calculate Bond Yield   151
Bond's Call Feature Can be Unfair   153
18. INCOME STOCKS   156
What is Your Stock Really Yielding Today?   156
19. GETTING THE DIVIDEND   159
Ex-Dividend Date is Key to Getting Dividend   159
20. THE DOW INDEX   162
How the Dow Jones Came to Be   162
21. ENTERING ORDERS   165
Correct Use of Stops, Limit and
    Market Orders   165

SECTION THREE:
YOUR INVESTMENT CHOICES   169
22. OPTIONS   171
Option Writing Involves Two Kinds of Risk   171
Option Writing for Income   173
23. MUTUAL FUNDS   176
Special Funds for Foreign Investors   176
Get the Right Money Market Fund   178
24. LIMITED PARTNERSHIPS   181
Inflation Fears Answered with Real Estate   181
Equipment Leasing Can Produce High Yield   183
25. BONDS   186
Premium Bonds Often Your Best Buy   186
26. GNMA   188
Ginnie Mae Can be a Heartbreaker   188
Little Known CMOs Have Terrific Features   190
27. TAX FREE   193
These Letters — AMT — Can Spell Higher
    Yields for You   193

28. UNIT TRUSTS   196
   Unit Trusts Make Convenient Package   196
29. ZERO-COUPON   198
   Zero-Coupon Securities Not Entirely Risk Free   198
30. COMMODITIES   201
   Trading in Commodities with Less Risk   201
   Obstacles to Overcome in Futures Trading   204
31. CONVERTIBLES   206
   Convertibles for Income and Growth   206
32. NEW PRODUCTS   209
   "Guaranteed Way" to be in the Stock Market   209
33. DEFERRED ANNUITIES   212
   Deferred Annuities Give Better Return
      than CDs   212
   Deferred Annuities for Safe Money Storage   214
   New CD-Annuity has it All   216

SECTION FOUR:
YOUR OWN PLAN   219
   Free Offer   221
   Contest Details   221
   Planning Your Estate   223

PREFACE

High up on the cliff overlooking the beautiful Amalfi Coast of Italy is a special village called Ravello. When you stand on your balcony, you can look out and see clouds passing through the valleys below you, mountains of every shape, and of course, the beautiful seacoast. But if you look right down, closer to where you are standing, you see the simple backyard of your villa, the deep green grass and the rich smelling roses. Somewhere about here, the commitment to spend the time to write this book was made.

This contrast, of the almost overpowering world around us and the simple basic things we see when we look closer, is the same in the world of finance. So, my hope is you will see no matter how complicated the world's finances appear, how simple it actually is to get control of your financial affairs. If you have never really had a chance to learn about money, this book is definitely for you.

I urge to take the time to get a better understanding of your finances. Reading *What Stockbrokers Don't Always Tell You* will give you an advantage not only in smart investing, but in dealing with other professionals in the legal and tax fields. When you read this book, you will be armed with the knowledge you need when you get together with your attorney, accountant or stockbroker.

You'll know when one of them is trying to lead you astray.

This book is written for those who want to know more about their money — making it grow and keeping more of it. To be successful I felt it had to be easy to read and loaded with helpful ideas you were not getting from those around you.

I organized the book into sections that cluster chapters of the same topics. You can read one chapter, or more, at a time. This way you can read on your coffee break, on your way into work, waiting for the mailman, on your next flight, or at the end of the day sitting in your favorite chair at home.

Each chapter is filled with ideas that can be used right away. For example, should you register your securities in joint or individual names? There are several chapters that deal with this question from different perspectives.

Who you choose to handle your financial affairs is one of the most critical decisions you will ever make. This book will protect you from the many unscrupulous thieves out there that see the business as a contest between your will and their egos.

To help you select the right person, you will find chapters dealing with choosing a broker. What qualities to look for and how to spot those characteristics. Other chapters will tell you what you should expect from a financial planner.

In another section, you get a look at stocks, bonds and some of Wall Street's newer products — from someone that is not trying to sell you any of them.

This book will help you see how easy it is to start taking control of your financial future.

If you do not have a will, I hope after reading the chapters on wills, you will put the book down and get started. If you need to know how to fund your retirement plan, you will learn what your best alternatives are when you get through reading those chapters.

You will find out once and for all how to figure out what you are worth, and how much estate tax your heirs might owe the IRS at your death. And then read the secret to arranging to pay this tax with a big discount.

In fact, I believe this is so important, that after reading the section on estate planning, if you would like me to tell you what amount of federal estate taxes you face, complete the forms on pages 223 to 227 and send them to me in care of the publisher. I will give you back an estate plan to follow that could save you tens or hundreds of thousands of dollars. See Section Four for further details.

Section Four also contains information on a special offer for those of you that believe you need to get all of your finances in order with a complete personal financial plan.

As with any book of this kind, you should take the information and advice and interpret it according to your own particular situation. Some of these ideas should be discussed with an attorney or accountant. State laws vary, and even the federal tax laws seem to be changing faster these days. Neither the publisher nor myself intend this book to be the final word.

SECTION ONE:
PLANNING YOUR FINANCES

CHAPTER 1
JOINT OWNERSHIP

WHEN NOT TO USE IT

One of the most popular questions asked at my, and I would imagine, any other financial planning seminar as well is, "How should we hold our stocks, bonds and other assets — in single name or joint tenancy?"

What is correct for you can only be determined after sitting down with a professional planner. However, here are some general guidelines that might help you.

For many people, joint ownership is very comfortable. Usually, a young married couple starting out acquires things such as a home, automobile, furniture, some stocks, etc., in joint name because they feel they acquired them together.

This is fine and good. Before divorce became so common, joint registration of property was almost 100 percent the case. Now it is not uncommon to see young couples, if both have careers, to keep some possessions in their own names.

As a general rule today, if your estate is worth a half million dollars or less, joint ownership may be right for you. Naturally, there could be other factors involved such as your ages, how well are you getting along with your spouse, or whether you want your half of the assets to go somewhere else. But, in general, joint ownership will mean that, at the death of one spouse, all of the assets will go to the other without any federal estate taxes or added expense and delay due to probate.

In larger estates, you should consider the advantages of holding your assets in separate names.

Here's why.

The Economy Recovery Tax Act of 1981 changed the marital deduction affecting your estate taxes at death. The new law allows spouses to transfer any and all assets to each other at death without any gift taxes. Thus, a million-dollar estate could be given at death from husband to wife without any federal estate taxes being paid to the government.

However, this balloons the size of the estate of the surviving spouse; and when he or she subsequently dies, the personal estate tax exception, currently at $600,000, will not be enough to cover the whole estate. A great deal of taxes will have to be paid.

This could be avoided by each spouse having assets registered in his or her name only and incorporating a trust. The trust can either be a living trust, which means it is established while the person is alive, or a testamentary trust, which is established after a person's death. Using this method, an individual can at his or her death pass an amount equal to their personal exemption of $600,000 to the trust, free of estate taxes, and the remainder to the spouse, using the marital deduction.

An important word of caution:

A growing number of people are learning this technique of passing on their estates with minimal or no estate tax. However, they are only partially doing what is necessary, and as a result, they are going to have some nasty surprises down the road.

It is not uncommon for me to come across a couple who say they have each made out a will that calls for such a trust arrangement allowing the surviving spouse to enjoy the income and the children to be the ultimate beneficiaries of the remaining assets.

So far, there is nothing wrong with that. But when I examine how they currently have their assets registered, I find everything is held jointly.

Guess what will happen at the time of death of the first spouse?

All of the assets, including those designed to go into the separate trust, will go over to the surviving spouse. This is fine if this is what they wanted. But, if they were trying to keep the size of the surviving spouse's estate below the higher tax levels, they failed.

Proper registration of your assets means removing the emotional importance of showing you own everything jointly, and registering those assets so at your death they will go where you want them, with the least amount of cost or delay.

JOINT TENANCY CAN LEAD TO TROUBLE

Registering your account at a brokerage firm in joint name is probably the most common way of registering an account. It eliminates probate, and there is a nice feeling about owning everything together with your spouse or loved one.

However, many times I have seen single people wanting to register their assets in joint names with someone else, not fully realizing the serious potential danger to which they are exposing themselves.

Here is an actual example with enough facts changed so no one will recognize the people involved.

Mr. and Mrs. Smith had an estate worth about $400,000. Everything was in joint name. When her husband died, Mrs. Smith took title to all the securities and the Smiths' house. There was no probate or estate taxes to pay.

Mrs. Smith has two stepdaughters from her marriage to Mr. Smith. One is 25 and in college. The other is 30 and is working in the same city as her stepmother.

Mrs. Smith gets along fine with her two stepdaughters and plans ultimately to leave the remaining estate at her death to both of them. However, Mrs. Smith is still somewhat new with the family, and the estate left her is all she has.

She is careful to draw up a new will, leaving everything to both stepdaughters equally. But to avoid probate, someone tells her she should re-register all her securities in joint name with her older stepdaughter, with joint right of survivorship. In turn, that stepdaughter will be responsible to divide the assets with her younger sister.

The strategy seems very practical at first glance. But there are potentially a couple of dangers.

First, our Mrs. Smith needs to be made aware that once she adds her stepdaughter's name on to the brokerage account with her, and they both sign the joint-account agreement, she has given her stepdaughter the right to, at anytime, call the office and instruct all the securities be sold and the proceeds be sent out to her.

The check would not even have to go out with both of their names on it. I doubt Mrs. Smith planned to give up this much control over her livelihood for the rest of her life.

And what if over the next couple of years there was a squabble between the two of them? Mrs. Smith would want to remove her stepdaughter's name from the account, no doubt. But how could she do this without her stepdaughter agreeing?

I do not have to go on. You can imagine your own terrible versions of this story.

Another factor Mrs. Smith needs to be made aware of is that her two stepdaughters may not always be as close as they are now. People change, and it is possible the two stepdaughters could grow apart. If all the assets were left to the oldest stepdaughter, even though there was a will saying she is to share everything with the younger stepdaughter, the assets held jointly by Mrs. Smith and the oldest stepdaughter would pass outside of the will, and the oldest stepdaughter could play finders-keepers, losers-weepers with her younger sister.

Maybe neither scenario would develop, but when money is involved, people change.

Here is a completely different story. This one has more tax implications to it, so, as always with tax matters, you should consult your accountant or tax attorney as well.

Mrs. Dale is widowed with one daughter. She has stocks and bonds totaling well over half a million dollars. At her death, she plans to leave everything to her sole daughter, Eileen.

So, Mrs. Dale, who insists in keeping all her securities in a bank vault, has all of the securities registered jointly with her daughter. This way, she reasons, when she passes away, Eileen will get all the securities and avoid probate at the same time.

Mrs. Dale probably has run afoul of the tax law, and she should go confess to her accountant. For, when you have securities registered in your name, and you add another person to make the securities jointly owned, you have immediately made a gift of half the value of the securities.

And remember, while the Economic Recovery Tax Act of 1981 allows husbands and wives to pass assets back and forth without incurring any gift tax, this favorable treatment does not apply to anyone else, including mother and daughter.

What Mrs. Dale probably should have done was to gift her daughter the $10,000 worth of securities each year she could, without any gift taxes, and have the rest of her securities brought into a brokerage firm.

Why?

Because thanks to a special gift tax rule, when the securities are held in street name at a brokerage firm, you can add another person's name to the account and no immediate transfer of property — therefore gift tax — is deemed to have occurred.

Granted, at a later date, if Eileen were to remove assets from that joint account, she would then trigger a taxable event. But at her mother's death, the assets would go to her without probate and be subject to an estate tax only on any excess over her mother's personal exemption.

There are different ways to register your account and pass assets on to your loved ones. Maybe a joint account is perfect for what you have in mind. On the other hand, ask someone to be sure.

CHAPTER 2
YOUR WILL

WILLS BEFORE 1981 COULD HAVE MAJOR FAULTS

A recent ruling by the IRS has made it clear: the provisions of your will shall be interpreted by the laws in effect at the time of its writing.

This means any married couple whose will was prepared and executed prior to September 12, 1981, need to have their will reviewed to be sure their assets will be shared as they planned, at the death of the first party.

You see, prior to the passage of the Economic Recovery Tax Act (ERTA) in 1981, the law said the amount of assets that could pass between husband and wife at death, free of federal estate taxes, could be no more than the greater of half of the adjusted gross estate of the deceased spouse or $250,000.

It was the ERTA that said there would be an unlimited marital deduction. That is to say, a decedent could leave their surviving spouse the entire estate and, because there is now an unlimited marital deduction, there would be no federal estate taxes to pay.

A will prepared before September 12, 1981, might contain language that says upon the death of that first spouse, the maximum marital deduction shall be taken, passing those assets to the surviving spouse. But remember, when that will was drawn, that language meant either half of the adjusted gross estate or $250,000.

But what about today? Could that language not be taken to mean pass everything? After all, that would be the maximum marital deduction.

Depending on the overall size of the estate or what was planned, that could alter the decedent's intentions.

For example, let us say the decedent planned to give part to his ex-wife and another part to the children. If that pre-1981 will is not changed, it could send everything to the wife and leave the children out completely.

Or take the case of a wife passing away and wanting to pass only part of her estate to her husband and leaving the rest in a trust providing him with additional income and the principal ultimately going to the children.

This technique is commonly used to avoid passing everything to the surviving spouse and leaving them with an estate way over the individual exemption of $600,000 we all enjoy.

But again, if this couple is not careful, all of the estate in her name will go to him and this could be much more than he will be able to pass over to the children using his personal exemption at his death.

So with all the new tax changes being bandied about, be sure to make an appointment to have your legal papers reviewed.

WILLS DON'T ALWAYS DO WHAT YOU WANT

Mary and Bob White have been living in a non-community property state, such as Florida, all their life. After paying their bills they never seem to have two nickels to rub together. And for a number of reasons, Mary and Bob have never really got along. In fact, they fight all the time.

But lo and behold, Mary White wins the state lottery and is suddenly worth more than a million dollars.

One of the first things she wants to do is fly up to Michigan to visit her favorite sister. Wary of plane travel, she writes a brief will leaving nothing to her husband and instead giving everything to her favorite sister. She has two people witness her will.

Question: Can Mary exclude Bob from her estate?

The answer, at least in a state such as Florida, is no. However, for that amount of money, it is a safe bet that the whole thing will end up in court. Bob should be able to win at least 30 percent of Mary's estate based on the state law where they reside that says neither spouse can totally disinherit their partner.

The law provides that in cases such as this, the disinherited spouse can step in and claim what is known as the elective share. In Florida, for instance, the elective share is 30 percent of the estate.

It is interesting to note that, prior to October, 1971, Florida law only protected a female spouse from being disinherited from her husband's estate. To get the latest standing of the law in your state, be sure to contact an attorney.

However, in cases where the surviving spouse has signed some type of antenuptial agreement and expressly waived his or her right to take a share of the estate, it is quite a different matter.

Here are some other wishes that you cannot be sure will be carried out, just because you put them in your will.

You can put in your will that you want a particular attorney to serve as attorney for your estate. And more than likely, your personal representative handling your affairs will honor your wishes. But, in fact, the decision to select a particular attorney is the decision of the personal representative and not the person that died. If that person wanted to use someone else who was legally and technically qualified, he or she could.

And certainly you cannot use a will to do something that is not legal.

For example, you could not say that you were leaving $100,000 to your daughter Brooke, but if she ever marries she will be disinherited. Certain things, like putting a restraint on marriage, are considered against the law.

Finally, many people specify in their wills that, upon their death, a trust be established. This trust might hold assets that are to go to their children and even further down the line to their grandchildren.

But there is a limit to how far the assets can be passed along. There is a rule against perpetuities. It says you cannot establish a trust in your will that runs longer than for the current beneficiaries plus 21 years and nine months.

These are just a few of the things a will cannot do. Of course, there are a lot of things a will can do. One thing for sure, as long as you are alive and competent, you can change a will all you want. But considering how important the language in your will is, I recommend you have your will prepared by a professional.

IMPORTANT REASONS FOR REVISING YOUR WILL

Chances are, whenever you sit down with an expert to prepare a financial plan, you will be asked whether you have a will.

My experience is that while most people will say they have a will, it was usually drawn up some years ago. And that can spell serious problems for your surviving spouse or other beneficiaries.

For example, let us say you have $800,000 in assets in your name you want to bequeath to your spouse. Your spouse has a similar amount. At your death, you would like to pass the $800,000 over to him or her and ultimately, to your children, with the least federal estate tax possible.

Chances are, if your will was drafted before the passage of the Economic Recovery Tax Act of 1981, you will have language in your will stating that you want to take maximum advantage of the marital deduction.

Sounds fine unless you remember prior to the passage of ERTA, the maximum marital deduction meant you could pass, tax free, the greater of $250,000, or one half of your estate to your spouse. In this case, it would be $400,000.

Today, however, that same language means the whole $800,000 will be passed to your spouse. The reason is, the marital deduction today is an unlimited one. Therefore, all of the $800,000 would be passed over to your spouse.

This could mean your spouse will have received more assets than he or she can pass on, tax free, at his or her demise. You should have used language leaving your spouse the amount in excess of that portion of your estate that qualifies for the credit shelter trust.

Here is another example I often see when working with out-of-towners.

A couple will come in and tell me that after visiting Florida for many years, they have retired or sold their business and wish to become Florida residents so they can benefit from the more favorable tax structure here.

In addition to advising the couple to register for voting in their new state and get their drivers licenses changed, I ask the couple when they last reviewed their will.

Many times, while the people's will might have been revised just a year ago, the very first paragraph of the will still says something like, "I, so- and- so, a resident of the State of Massachusetts . . . ."

In these days of federal government support being withdrawn and states under increasing pressure to find ways to beef up their treasuries, it would not take much for your old state to come waving your will and looking for some taxes.

Sure, your personal representative can go to court and fight back showing ample evidence to the contrary. But, why take the risk? Take care of it right now. Have your will reviewed by an attorney living in your newly adopted state.

You should also have your will reviewed if you decide to add or remove a beneficiary. Likewise, if you change your mind about the amount you are going to leave someone.

Perhaps the person you named to handle your affairs has died, or, for whatever reason, you wish to name someone else to act as your personal representative.

Fortunately, in many cases, these changes will not be too involved and an attorney can make them with a codicil to your existing will.

THINGS TO CONSIDER BEFORE SEEING THE ATTORNEY

Going through my mail recently, I came across a concise, yet useful, booklet on preparing or reviewing your will.

The booklet is called, "What to do Before Drafting or Reviewing Your Will," and is put out by a local community hospital foundation office. I am sure you could contact a hospital or college near you for a similar pamphlet.

The booklet stresses that your attorney can do a better job for you and at less cost if you are prepared before you meet with him or her.

It points out that your attorney cannot draw up your will on hunches. To do a complete job, not only making sure you have legally provided for the transfer of your estate, but also have saved on estate taxes and met all of your beneficiary needs, you will have to tell your lawyer not only the financial details of your life but also any relevant personal facts.

For example, you will have to let the attorney know about any previous marriages that may still be a factor in how your finances are to be disposed. Is there a prenuptial agreement? Do any of your planned beneficiaries suffer from major mental or physical handicaps?

Where do you want your assets to go at your death? To your spouse? Children? Relatives? A charity? In what amounts?

I should mention that although an attorney will be the one to draw up your will, financial and estate planners often include as part of their service, helping you gather all of the facts and determining with you what you want your will to say before you even walk into the attorney's office. It just depends on whom you are most comfortable working with or who you feel knows you better.

Either way, this booklet should be helpful in showing you what areas of your life you should have documented before seeing your attorney.

For example, the booklet tells you to list your assets — such as a home, a second home, bank accounts, securities, annuities and pension plans and to put down their approximate worth today. Also, indicate whether the assets are jointly owned by you and your spouse or individually. This is important.

Federal estate tax law provides that anyone, at his or

her death, can leave an estate worth $600,000 and pay no federal estate taxes. In addition, a married couple can leave one another any amount and not be concerned about having to pay taxes on the transfer.

So generally speaking, if your estate is less than $600,000, you can probably register all of your securities in joint name with your spouse and avoid any probate or estate taxes at the death of the first spouse. Subsequently, when the surviving spouse dies, estate taxes can again be avoided through the $600,000 personal exemption.

However, if after tallying your assets, you find your estate is worth considerably more than the $600,000 federal allowance, you will want to consider splitting up ownership of the assets to save on estate taxes. Owning property under a single name brings up the problem of probate, but that can generally be solved by using a living trust.

The booklet goes on to ask whether you have given much thought to how you want your assets distributed upon your death and whether the person receiving your holdings will be able to cope with the situation.

For example, you plan to leave everything to your spouse at your death. Is he or she going to be able to manage those assets wisely? Does your spouse have the experience or the health to do a good job? And what if you have very young children and both you and your spouse die at an early age? Minor children cannot be responsible for managing the assets you leave behind. You should name someone, either a person or corporation, that will step in under those circumstances to manage things.

Then again, you may have a favorite charity you would like to leave something to, for the help they have given you or to be sure their good works will go on.

If this is the case, you will want to discuss with your planner whether the gift should be made at your death or whether it would be advantageous for you to set up the gift now using one of the different charitable trusts, such as a charitable remainder trust. This plan will give your beneficiaries income from the assets for the rest of their lives, and then they can pass the assets over to the charity. That means tax savings to you and a benefit to your chosen charity.

Of course, a number of different circumstances could affect the plan you devise. You may want to spend a little time and money and discuss the plan with a professional.

You know the old saying, some things can be put off but death and taxes will come. You owe it to yourself and your heirs to make sure you have a proper will.

CHAPTER 3
SAVING ON ESTATE TAXES

HOW TO GET UP TO A 90% DISCOUNT

Imagine getting a discount on the biggest tax bill you might ever get in your life.

As unbelievable as that may seem, there is enough truth to this that, for the sake of your spouse or other loved ones, you should find out whether you, too, can get a discount of 50 to 90 percent on your estate taxes!

Each year on April 15, you get a tax bill that you have no choice but to pay. Then, as if you have not been taxed enough during your life, at death the government levies an estate tax. And if you thought paying 15 or 28 percent tax on your income was bad, consider that tax rates on your estate can go as high as 55 percent.

Fortunately, under the tax code, the federal government gives us an allowance against some of these taxes.

Each of us, as an individual, is able to bequeath up to $600,000 to beneficiaries at death without any federal estate taxes. This means, using rather simple estate planning strategies, a husband and wife can pass $1.2 million dollars on to their children without any federal estate taxes. But, for each dollar beyond these amounts, the IRS stands ready with a tax bill: due in full, in cash, nine months after death.

But did you know that you can often pre-arrange to have your heirs pay off the potentially whopping tax bite with a discount of 50 percent or more?

So, if you have exhausted all of the estate planning strategies and you find you still have a large tax bill that is going to reduce the amount you can leave your spouse, or children, you need to continue with the estate-planning tax-savings process and see whether some estate settlement insurance can save you dollars. Do not get scared by the fact that insurance is involved.

In the past you purchased insurance on your life so if you died prematurely, your family would have the funds to see the children could still go off to college, etc. And you buy automobile insurance in case you are in an accident. You purchase insurance like that hoping you will never have to use it.

This is different. In this case, you already know you will be using the insurance.

And in case you are thinking you do not need the insurance because you are already leaving plenty for your loved ones, consider the following example:

If you left an estate of $1 million for your spouse, and he or she spent $100,000 a year, increasing the amount five percent a year to offset inflation, and the rest of the money sat in an account earning 10 percent after taxes, guess how long it would be before your spouse was completely broke?

Fourteen years. The lesson is, you can never leave too much.

For starters, find out just what your estate tax bill will be by going to someone experienced in estate work. It could be an accountant, attorney, insurance agent, trust officer or other financial advisor. (Remember, as part of buying this book, I will do this for you free. Just complete the form in Section Four.) If it looks as though your estate is going to be in for some heavy taxes, then you can try to determine whether purchasing some of this joint and last survivorship insurance I refer to as estate settlement insurance, will work for you.

Here is a recent example.

A couple in their early 60's had an estate including stocks, bonds, pension, home, etc., of $2.3 million. Even with planning so each of them will take advantage of their $600,000 exemption, there was a federal estate tax due of about $370,000 that the children would have to pay within nine months of their parents' death.

But by matching up the right insurance policy, our client was able to arrange for $370,000 death benefit coverage to go to the children to pay the tax in full by spending about $70,000. That represents a saving of 80 percent!

It is important to select the right insurance and set it up properly so you will not inadvertently add to your estate tax problem. But, depending on your situation, the savings can be startling.

FLOWER BONDS BLOSSOM AT DEATH

It is not a subject you like to bring up with clients, and writing about it is not much easier. Who wants to talk about death and taxes?

However, when you are involved in planning someone's estate or if you are planning your own affairs, you really should know about what are sometimes called Flower Bonds, or to put it a little more directly, Death Bonds.

These bonds have only one function as far as you and I are concerned. They are purchased by someone anticipating death, that is, someone who can hear death rapping at the front door.

These bonds, which are actually U.S. Treasury bonds, pay as little as 3 to 4 percent, and therefore sell at a discount from their face value. But while they have little income value, you will see, they have a great potential tax benefit.

When someone dies, the personal representative files tax form 706 to show the value of the estate. To make sure nothing is left out, the IRS publishes a guide, almost as thick as the form itself, to make the personal representative's task "easier".

Taxes on an estate can go as high as 55 percent. When you consider there may be additional charges and fees, such as court costs, appraisal fees and possibly probate, you can see why financial and estate planning get so much attention.

It is against the federal estate tax that is due, that Flower Bonds, those special government securities with the engraving of flowers on the back side, get their "blossoming power."

The IRS has ruled that, for estate tax purposes, the bonds must be included in the estate at their face redemption value, rather than their cost. This means a bond that was purchased just a short time ago at a discount because of its low rate of interest is accepted at face value in paying estate taxes.

An example of one of these Flower Bonds would be the 3 1/2's due in 1998. They can be purchased in denominations ranging from $500 to $100,000. You can get a complete list of the bonds available by contacting any Federal Reserve bank or branch. You can get current quotes by calling your broker.

When you consider the coupons on these bonds are small, you can understand why it is very important not to buy too many. That is why if you are thinking of purchasing some of these Flower Bonds, you should consult your accountant or tax attorney first.

Although the law allows you to purchase these bonds

virtually on your deathbed, you must be sure they are purchased properly and executed while the person dying is of clear mind.

The IRS has ruled that ownership must be documented by a transfer of title, accompanied by assignment and delivery — if in registered form — or by delivery, if in bearer form. When you call your broker, the trade date on your confirmation receipt satisfies the delivery requirement, even though actual delivery does not take place until weeks later.

CHAPTER 4
TRUSTS

TRUSTS FOR SECOND MARRIAGES

A Q-tip is a handy tool. So is a trust vehicle carrying the same name.

When the Economic Recovery Tax Act was signed in 1981, the part of the act changing the marital deduction altered another very important provision at the same time.

In the past, unless a surviving spouse could prove he or she actually contributed money into building up the family's estate, the marital deduction that could be taken to reduce the size of the taxable estate at the death of one of the spouses was half the adjusted gross estate, or $250,000, whichever was greater.

For example, Mr. and Mrs. Smith have an adjusted gross estate worth $800,000. This includes a home up north and a second home in the south, stocks, bonds, jewelry, and so forth. Let us say Mr. Smith dies first. Under prior law, Mr. Smith would pass to Mrs. Smith a marital deduction of half of the estate, or $400,000, in order to reduce the size of Mr. Smith's estate before calculating the estate taxes.

However, here is the key point. The law said, for the Smiths to get away with reducing the estate by giving

$400,000 to his wife, Mr. Smith had to give up any say about how that money would be disposed of at his wife's death.

Theoretically, several years later, Mrs. Smith would die and the remaining assets she got from the estate would be passed down to their children.

Fine and good.

Except what if this was a second marriage for one or both of the Smiths, and there were children involved from a prior marriage? Can Mr. Smith be sure assets passed over to his wife will go to his children upon her death? Maybe she really did not get along with the children that well and, instead, at her death she passes the remaining assets to her children from a prior marriage.

And don't think that has not happened.

Or, what if Mrs. Smith remarries and later divorces? Is there not a danger that a lot of the assets would be dissipated in a divorce settlement and not reach the children as Mr. Smith intended? Naturally, this works both ways. Mrs. Smith could be afraid if she died first and left a large part of the estate to Mr. Smith, he might run off with some "young thing" and soon find himself in a financial mess.

Well, ERTA contains language that can prevent this situation.

First, to make it easier to reduce the estate tax and get around the problem of how much each of the spouses contributed to the building up of the family's estate, the law now says a husband and wife can pass assets to each other without any estate or gift tax being involved.

If we return to our example of the Smiths, Mr. Smith can actually pass the whole estate of $800,000 to Mrs. Smith and there would be no federal estate tax.

Now, that probably would not be a good idea because it could lead to greater taxes being due when Mrs. Smith dies. However, for the point we want to make, let us assume that he intends to give everything to Mrs. Smith.

In the past, to get such an absolute tax break, he had to give up control of how she could dispose of the estate at her death.

But now, under the law, assets can be passed over to a surviving spouse and the marital deduction can be claimed without relinquishing complete control of these assets.

The assets are now being transferred, giving the surviving spouse what is called a qualified terminable interest in the property. This is done under an arrangement called a Q-TIP trust.

Basically, the trust allows the surviving spouse to enjoy the income from the assets that were passed over to him or her and even invade the principal to a modest degree, if necessary, but not to control the disbursement of those assets at death.

TRUSTS FOR SINGLE PEOPLE

So much is written today about saving money on your estate taxes. A lot of the advice revolves around setting up a marital trust and a residuary trust at the death of the first spouse.

But what about the person who is single?

At the seminars I give, I tell married couples to plan as early as possible so they can take advantage of the marital deduction. But often some single person will raise his or her hand and say, "What about me?"

"When my spouse passed away, everything was left to me," the person says. "We did not have to pay any federal estate taxes, because as you say, we used the unlimited marital deduction. But now I have an estate worth close to three quarters of a million dollars. If I do not do some effective planning, much of my estate will never get past the tax man."

These people are so right. While the individual estate allowance allows you to bequeath $600,000 free of federal estate taxes, the amount over that figure will be taxed at up to 55 percent.

What can be done?

Well, naturally each situation should be analyzed carefully. You need to let your adviser know where you would like to pass your assets. Children? Grandchildren? Will they be able to manage the money you leave them? Might you be thinking of leaving some money to one or two charities? How is your health? Have you provided for yourself should you become incapacitated for a long time?

Knowing you, and what you would like to do with your assets, will help your adviser structure a plan for you to reduce or possibly eliminate completely any federal estate taxes at your death.

For example, you may be able to make lifetime gifts or set up charitable trusts that will serve you or your heirs.

We are allowed by law to give up to $10,000 to as many people as we like without having to pay a gift tax. So, a program can be set up right now to give as much as $10,000 each year to all those individuals you plan to leave your estate to anyway. If the individual is too young to handle the money, a trust could be set up to manage the money.

You might want to give special consideration to assets in your possession that are liable to increase substantially over the next number of years.

For example, say you have a stock that might appreciate from $10,000 to $20,000 over the next five years. If you give it away now, you escape gift taxes. If you waited you may have another $10,000 still in your estate exposed to taxation.

Some advisers suggest you make use of a grantor trust.

These vehicles can be set up by you to pay you a certain sum over their length of existence, whether it is 10 years, 15 years, or whatever. If you outlive the length of the trust, the remaining amount passes to whom you designated, without any tax.

Charitable lead trusts and charitable remainder trusts offer yet other methods to avoid taxes on an estate.

With these trusts you will be helping a worthy organization, saving on estate taxes by getting assets out of your estate, and also saving on current income taxes by making a charitable gift.

The charitable remainder trust makes payments to you, and if you design it such, to another person, during your and their lifetime. At the death of both of you the remainder in the trust goes to the charity.

The charitable lead trust works a little differently.

In this case, the assets in the trust make payments to the charity. Then after a certain length of time, the trust expires, and the assets are passed to those you designated.

For example, right now you may have some assets that you do not need for your support. You can place them into a charitable lead trust for the benefit of the charity, and after a certain length of time, the assets can be transferred over to your children.

No question, without the marital deduction, it is more difficult to develop a plan to save on estate taxes. However, if you have a large estate and you wish to pass on as much as possible to your beneficiaries, approaches are available to you.

PLACING YOUR TRUST IN A TRUST

I have pointed out some of the things a will was not

good at doing. Now we will cover one of the major reasons a growing number of Americans are turning to trusts as part of their financial plan.

A trust can give you control of the assets you leave behind.

For example, say you have two children to whom you plan to leave everything at your death. One child is sensible about money. The other, however, does not seem to appreciate the value of a dollar, and you are afraid he may burn through his inheritance.

Or you would like to leave money for your children or grandchildren to finish college. But what if one of the children really does not want to go to college. Perhaps this child has an opportunity to be financially successful in another endeavor but needs some start-up money.

If your will says that child gets no money unless he or she goes on to college, your personal representative might be prohibited from doing anything for that child.

Another scenario that is all too common these days is where you plan to leave a large settlement to your son or daughter. However, the marriage does not look too solid to you. You are afraid money left to your son or daughter will be commingled and if there is a divorce soon, your child could stand to lose much of what you left him or her.

These are just some of the problems a simple trust vehicle, properly prepared by legal counsel, can solve. People are learning that if they do not want to have all the assets they worked so hard to accumulate squandered overnight, they had better make plans about how to control those assets after they are gone.

There are actually many different kinds of trusts. For the last number of years I have been pointing out the value of a Qualified Terminal Interest Property trust — Q-TIP for short. This interesting trust can solve a lot of family squabbles.

A couple gets married for the second time. Let us say one of the two is bringing most of the wealth into the marriage. There are children from the first marriage on both sides.

Typically, the couple will agree that their combined assets should be used for their enjoyment. And at the death of one, the combined assets should continue to provide income for the survivor.

However, the party bringing in the bulk of the assets probably is going to say that after the death of his or her spouse, he or she would like the remaining assets to go to his or her children and not to the children of the other spouse.

Sounds good. But we know all too well that when death occurs, people change, and promises that were made are often times broken.

This is where the Q-TIP trust can come in to save the day. This trust allows one spouse to pass assets over to a surviving spouse for their maintenance and health without any federal estate taxes, but the surviving spouse in this case cannot control where the assets will go after his or her demise. That has been predetermined by the first spouse by setting up the Q-TIP trust.

A final example. In this case, the client is a widow that may or may not have children. Right now, she is capable of managing her affairs, but she is concerned that a few years from now, she may become incapacitated and need someone to come in and help her. She does not want to go into a nursing home.

She may have made this point very clear to her children or other relatives. But when the time comes that she does have difficulty taking care of herself, she may find those appointed to serve as her guardian and to be the ultimate beneficiaries of her remaining estate may commit her to a nursing home where it will be much less expensive to keep her.

These are just a sampling of the situations a trust can help solve.

CHAPTER 5
ESTATE PLANNING STRATEGIES

ESTATE PLANNING FOR THE NOT SO RICH

When we see the word estate, as in estate planning, many people tend to think it only applies to the very wealthy.

Not only are these people incorrect, but, by thinking that, they may be cheating their spouse or children.

Unfortunately, it is a fact, so many of the same loving, caring people who struggle and work so hard during their lifetime to acquire and build up some extra assets so they can be sure their surviving spouse or children will not be "financially abandoned" after their death, never quite get around to planning their estate.

Maybe it is because it is so easy to put off things that we believe can be done tomorrow, or perhaps it is just a mistaken belief that developing an estate plan will have no real benefit to those surviving.

But whatever the reason, if you even suspect you may have an estate that either is quite large or has what you believe are special circumstances, get someone to look at it.

Let us take a look at some different people in various

circumstances I see quite often. See if you recognize any of these people's circumstances.

The widow or widower who either has no children or children who live somewhere else, or in any event, have their own lives. Perhaps these people fear as they get older they may be pushed into living in a home for the elderly, even though they have the assets to allow them to stay where they are even if it means hiring special help.

People in this position should investigate creating a living trust.

In the trust, they could require that in the event they become incapable of taking care of themselves, rather than be placed in a home or sent to live with someone they really do not want to, a previously named trustee they had standing by for this kind of event, will step in. The named trustee will make sure they go on living where they want to and that all the bills, etc., will be taken care of by the trustee.

What about people who have a second or third marriage?

In many of these cases, the new couple agrees to pool their money to enhance their living style and may even decide at the death of one, the combined assets should continue to go to support the survivor.

However, when the surviving spouse dies, each member of the couple wants the assets to be distributed to members on their side of the family. Similarly, should the surviving spouse remarry, the assets are not to be commingled into the new relationship.

These are very common sentiments. But, sometimes, they are not openly discussed because people are afraid to open a can of worms. They don't know there is a relatively easy way to achieve exactly what they want.

One last example: A young couple with very young children.

The husband and wife are bright, hard working and have gone as far as to create wills that leave everything to the other at death. And, should they both die in something like a plane crash, they have named in their wills the person they want to look after their children.

Sounds pretty good. They have certainly taken steps along the right road. Could their planning be improved? Perhaps.

It could be 10 or 15 years before those children reach the age of majority. That is a long time. The person or persons named to look after the children may move, change their living style, become financially ruined or die. In other words, circumstances change.

Or perhaps the guardians will do a good job, but one or all the children will immediately claim what is left from the estate once they reach the age of majority. It may not even be a whole lot of money, but if the children have little experience in handling money, they may go through it before thinking of extra schooling or buying a house, and so forth.

Again, you can take steps now with correct wording in a trust to head off some of these possible problems.

You should arrange to meet someone who is involved with estate planning. That could be an attorney specializing in estates and wills, an insurance specialist in the same area, a financial planner, an accountant or bank trust officer. You will find they will be happy to talk with you without cost or obligation — at least for the first visit.

CHOOSING THE RIGHT EVALUATION DATE

If someone asks you to serve as the executor of an estate, or personal representative as some states such as Florida prefer to use, you might want to say thanks but no thanks.

Besides it taking more time than you imagined, there is the emotional matter of distributing someone's personal property to the other loved ones, who may now argue what Mom or Dad really meant in their wills. And then there are the legal and tax questions.

It is no wonder many financial advisors suggest a corporate executor, such as a trust department, be named personal representative of an estate or at least co-personal representative.

Let us address just one decision that might be involved. The decision by the personal representative about whether the estate should be valued on the date of death or, if it qualifies, six months later.

This decision, if made thoughtlessly, could carry heavy repercussions.

It is this decision that determines the cost basis of the assets that are being passed to beneficiaries. Cost basis is the figure your accountant needs when you sell or otherwise dispose of something, so he or she can calculate whether you did it at a gain or loss. Uncle Sam likes to know these things.

For many years, you were able to take either the date of death or the date six months later as the date you used to establish the cost basis. But that was changed by Congress with the passage of the 1984 Tax Reform Act.

Now, the law says a personal representative of an estate can elect to use the alternate valuation date six months later only if an estate tax return is required to be filed; that is, if an estate tax is owed.

So, if someone is passing an estate that is $600,000 or less, there is no federal estate tax due, and, therefore, no option of using the alternate valuation date.

Similarly, someone passing an estate of any size to a spouse who will claim that unlimited marital deduction cannot use the alternate date.

However, even if estate taxes are due, a second qualification deems that you can opt for the secondary date only if that results in the total gross estate and the resultant estate taxes being lower than at the date of death.

Let's take an example.

Abe dies, leaving an estate worth $700,000. It is made up of a condominium fully paid for, some personal property, jewelry and clothes — and several hundred thousand dollars of tax-free bonds, common stocks, and a money market fund.

An estate tax will be owed, because it is over the $600,000 level and Abe was not married at the time of his death, so he cannot use the marital deduction. Had Abe's estate been able to avoid estate taxes, his personal representative would have had no choice but to take the date of death as the date for asset valuation.

The lower the value of his estate, the less tax that will have to be paid and the more that can be shared among beneficiaries.

But, this is a case in which what is good for the goose is not always good for the gander. If you are inheriting some of the estate, you would want to get the property at the highest valuation possible so that, in the future, if you dispose of the condominium or securities, you will have little or no taxable gain to show.

Let us say you inherit 100 shares of General Motors at $70 a share. If you sell it for $75 a share, you have a taxable gain of $5 a share, or $500. But, if you inherit the stock when the market is down, and your cost basis is $50 a share, when you sell the stock for $75 a share, you owe taxes on a gain of $25 a share, or $2,500. Both ways, you took in $7,500 when you sold the stock, but in the second example, you will have a lot bigger tax to pay on your profit.

In other words, if General Motors is selling at $70 a share when Abe died, and six months later it is selling at $50 a share, by choosing the later date, Abe's estate will be worth less and the estate tax will be less. You, on the other hand, will probably be faced with a bigger tax bite. But, Congress feels you still got something for nothing.

By looking more closely at the law, we see it is the value of the total gross estate that must decrease to qualify for the second date. Not every item must go down. Here is where proper planning with your tax attorney and accountant can be worth 10 times their fee.

It is possible in six months that the stock market could fall so that the estate is decreased, although the condominium Abe owned has gone up dramatically because it was in a super location.

You could choose the later date and distribute the much-appreciated condominium to someone in a high tax bracket who plans to sell it right away, thus avoiding capital gains taxes on the appreciation. Then distribute the securities to beneficiaries that are in a lower tax bracket, like young children, so they could collect dividends for years and, when the market is up again, sell the securities. Being in a lower tax bracket, they will pay less in taxes on the gain. Depending upon the beneficiaries and the assets involved, many combinations could be tried.

You can see why it is not a job for an amateur.

CORRECT PLANNING FOR INSURANCE BENEFITS AT DEATH

Part of total estate planning is making sure as much of your estate as possible goes to your beneficiaries and not into the general coffers of the government.

In this regard, one of the key areas often overlooked is

the amount of insurance proceeds payable at death and to whom they are payable.

Careless handling of this asset can lead to delays in payments being made, extra taxes reducing the amount, and perhaps claims by people you do not want to profit by your death.

But in working with many cases, it is not uncommon to find situations like this example.

Mr. and Mrs. Goldman have carefully registered all their bank accounts and securities totaling $400,000 in joint name. At the death of either, the survivor will inherit all these assets without any probate or federal estate taxes. Sounds like they did their homework until we remind them, they own a home jointly, and that will be worth another $200,000 to the survivor and that Mr. Goldman has an insurance policy that will pay to Mrs. Goldman another $500,000 at his death.

In effect, if Mr. Goldman dies first, Mrs. Goldman will have an estate worth, not $400,000 — an amount easily passed over to their children at her death without estate taxes — but instead, an estate worth $1.1 million. And to pass that over to the children will result in a whole lot of estate taxes.

Here is another problem that some people with large insurance policies might experience.

They plan to leave the proceeds of a rather large insurance policy to several relatives. They have the insurance policy name one relative as the beneficiary, so the proceeds can pass free of probate. But, now how can they ever really be sure the beneficiary will follow through on their wishes in distributing the money to the other relatives?

These are ways to solve both of these problems, but first, let us backtrack just a little.

One of the nice things about insurance is that the

proceeds are received by the person named as beneficiary, without their having to pay any income tax. Also, because insurance passes to the beneficiary as a result of the wording in the insurance contract and not because of what a person's will says, there is no probate involved.

By the way, you may want to reread that paragraph.

So many times, we come across situations where a person says they want all their money to go to a specific person and have their will written this way, only to forget their insurance policy names someone else as the beneficiary. And those insurance proceeds are going to that person named as beneficiary no matter what the will says. So, especially if you have had any changes in your life, such as divorce, be sure you review to whom your insurance is payable.

Okay, moving on. With insurance, we see we can leave money to someone else without them having to pay taxes on the money, and there is no probate. However, because we still own and control the insurance policy, those dollars will be included in our estate and will be subject to federal estate tax.

In the case of a married couple, the solution is often as simple as making the spouse the beneficiary rather than the estate of the person that is insured. This is because the law allows us to pass any amount of money to our spouse without incurring any estate taxes. But sometimes this creates a problem such as that experienced by the Smiths.

Well, if we do not want to leave the insurance death benefit to a spouse for fear of ballooning their estate beyond what the federal estate tax exemption is, and we do not want to leave it to our estate because that could subject it to estate taxes, what do we do?

For one, you could ask your tax attorney or other financial adviser about the value of setting up an insurance trust.

When you transfer your policy to a trust it is as though you assigned it over to an individual. There are requirements, including: 1) the trust needs to be irrevocable; 2) you need to live at least three years after giving up control of the policy; 3) there could be gift taxes as a consequence.

But establishing an insurance trust will avoid having those dollars taxed in your estate and there will be no probate. If there are a number of relatives, perhaps some of them minors, the trust will be sure to carry out your instructions as to the disposition of the funds.

You can also set up the trust to pay the income that money can earn to your surviving spouse for life, and then at his or her death, the trust can terminate and pass the remaining assets to the children. This way, the spouse has had the advantages of the assets in the trust without having them included in his or her estate.

CORRECT USE OF POWERS OF ATTORNEY

There is a simple legal instrument available in some states, such as Florida, that will allow residents to maintain control over their assets, yet allow someone to step in and handle their affairs if they become incapacitated.

It is called a durable family power of attorney.

Do not confuse this with common law power of attorney which gives someone the right to act for someone else under certain circumstances.

For example, a specific power of attorney can be established so that an individual can be designated to act for someone else on a single given occasion. For example, if someone has to be out-of-town during the closing of a house, he or she can appoint a representative to sign documents in his or her absence.

Some people even execute what is referred to as a

general power of attorney. This power is much broader in authority and gives the holder of the power of attorney authority to act for the other person in all kinds of matters.

The problem with these powers of attorney, however, is that — at least, in most instances — they become invalid at the moment the person who gave the power becomes incapacitated or dies.

One can easily see, then, the problem of using the common law power of attorney when it comes to planning estates that seek to protect the individual when he or she becomes sick or injured or grows old. Just when the power is needed, it becomes null and void.

In response, some states, including Florida, have what is termed a durable power of attorney. In Florida, the word "family" is added because the state statute restricts the option to certain specified family members only.

This kind of power of attorney does not terminate when the person who delegated it becomes incapacitated in some way. However, if a court finds the person incompetent and appoints a guardian, then all powers of attorney, including a durable power, are void.

Let us look at a couple of examples.

Mr. and Mrs. Brown have an estate worth $400,000. It includes their home, two cars, some stocks and bonds and a savings account. They each have a will that leaves everything to the other. To avoid probate as much as possible, they have registered their assets in joint name with right of survivorship.

Many people would think the Browns are all set. They are avoiding federal estate taxes and probate. But something is missing.

What if Mrs. Brown is injured in an automobile accident and becomes incapacitated as a result? Her husband would probably have to petition the court to be able to sell securities, raise money, or pay bills, because all of the assets are registered in both names, and Mrs. Brown is in no condition to sign anything.

If the Browns had a durable family power of attorney giving each the right to act for the other should one become incapacitated, this problem would be avoided.

Here is a more common example.

Mrs. Weinstein is a widow with two children. She has an estate worth about $300,000 and figures this is enough to take care of her for the rest of her life. Though she plans to leave everything to her two children at her death, she does not like the idea of giving up control of her assets by making joint accounts with her children while she is alive.

Still, she is concerned that, at her advanced age, she could suffer a stroke or otherwise suddenly be incapacitated. What would happen to her? Would the children be able to use her assets to pay her bills and get her the care she needs?

Actually, the children probably would be able to get access to her assets, but only after going to court and being appointed her guardians. It is even possible the children would have to go back to court every time a large amount of money was needed. And each trip before the judge would cost money that could better be spent on Mrs. Weinstein.

If you find yourself in a situation similar to Mrs. Weinstein's, you can prevent this problem by having a durable family power of attorney which says your children are allowed to use your assets and make other legal and financial decisions for you.

As with other legal procedures, you should talk with your attorney before executing such a broad power as power of attorney.

CHAPTER 6
FINANCIAL PLANNING

A GOOD FINANCIAL PLAN IS YOUR KEY TO SUCCESS

In the world of money and finance, one of the key phrases today is financial planning.

Everyone from the big firms on Wall Street to the small, one-person office sitting in some strip shopping center is offering financial planning these days. This service has evolved as a result of the upheaval in the financial services industry.

Today, everyone seems to be moving into everyone else's territory. Savings and loans are making car loans; banks can now sell stock, and your stockbroker is telling you about the better checking account he can offer you.

In recent years, the rules governing your IRA have changed. So have the laws involving your will, marital deduction and how your estate will be taxed.

You walk into a brokerage office and announce you want to purchase some tax free bonds. Simple, right? But, do you want long-term or short-term? Discount, or at a premium? Do you want them in a unit trust, a mutual fund or individually? What quality rating are you looking for? Do you want insured bonds or not?

The proliferation of new financial products has been mind-boggling. With all the choices comes the need for better planning.

Perhaps we can define financial planning something like this. It is taking a unified approach to all of your finances so you will be better able to organize your assets to maximize your growth or your income, while minimizing your tax burden so that you may have a better chance of reaching your goals.

It is a shame, but we spend so much time and effort in earning money so we can do the things we want, and yet so little time in managing the assets we already have accumulated.

For instance, many people believe if they could just earn another $5,000 this year, that would solve their problems. However, even if they managed to increase their salary by that amount, they would soon look back and find they are in the same predicament. Many times, with proper planning, a couple could find that $5,000 within their existing income.

So you see, financial planning should not be regarded as just for the very wealthy. In fact, financial planning can help almost anyone. It can help:

* A young couple in the accumulative phase of their financial life.

* A busy person whose time is taken up with business and career matters, leaving personal financial management unattended.

* An individual or family experiencing increasing tax liabilities.

* An individual or family considering a major purchase or sale of a substantial asset, such as stock or a residence.

* A couple or individual about to retire.

* A spouse suddenly left alone either because of death or divorce.

* Anyone searching for an objective

approach to coordinating his or her financial affairs.

But understand: when I say financial planning is the key to the above cases, I mean the financial planning process. I personally do not think you have to see only someone that is a member of the International Association of Financial Planners, or is a Certified Financial Planner, or Registered Financial Planner. While any or all of these designations tell you the person is interested in holding themselves out to be planners, it does not necessarily mean they will do a good job for you.

Now let us talk about how to select a good planner, what you should expect him or her to do for you, and how you can get the most out of planning.

WHAT TO EXPECT FROM A GOOD PLANNER

It is 2:30 p.m. and you are probably just a little bit apprehensive. You are wondering why you agreed to the appointment in the first place. But here you are, about to meet with what could be your future financial planner.

We have already discussed how financial planning has been growing in popularity and why you should make use of it. Rather than doing things piecemeal, through financial planning, you can maximize your assets to achieve your goals in a unified way.

So, you have selected the person you think might do a good job, and now you are wondering just what is going to happen.

The first thing you can expect is that you will not be sold any investments. So relax! For a good planner to plan, he or she will first need information from you.

To me, this data gathering session has two functions. One is the collection of hard data and the other is to see how you think and react. This latter function, the development of empathy between planner and client, means talking about family members, level of risk tolerance, possible scars from divorce, the Great Depression or whatever.

To gather the hard data, many planners will use a questionnaire. Others will not, because they feel it is too structured. These planners prefer to make continuous notes during the interview.

Either way, you can be expected to reveal what your income is from salary, as well as from other sources, such as a membership on a board of directors or a part-time position you hold several days a week. Other questions will be asked. Where is your money at present? In stocks? Which ones? How long have you held them? When will they mature?

What are your monthly expenses? Are there any unusual expenses coming up we will have to plan for? Are the children going to college? Do you plan to pay for it? Is this your first marriage or has there been another, or others? Are you paying alimony? Do you support other members of your family?

Very often, a full interview like this can last a couple of hours. To assist in getting the correct information, I often suggest people bring in their last two income tax returns, their insurance policies, as well as any other documents that might be helpful.

Out of this information gathering and general conversation must come your financial goals. You probably will have several goals. Some will probably be short term, like sheltering your taxable income this year, so you pay less taxes, and some might be long term, like making sure the money is there to help send your two children to college in eight and ten years.

If you are recently retired, in many ways your situation

is easier to plan. There are fewer variables, and, if you are like most people, your major goal is to make sure you do not have to change your lifestyle down the road, because taxes and inflation have eaten into your present nest egg. Also very important to you will probably be how you can pass the most wealth to your surviving spouse, and then on to the children.

Armed with all this information, your planner will formulate your plan after a couple of weeks of digesting all the information.

That could encompass, depending on your situation, a restatement of your goals so that you know that you and your advisor are working toward the same end. The plan should also deal with cash flow and include a review of your investments.

It should answer your questions on how to reduce your taxes, and review your insurance coverage and your retirement plan. It also could include a review of your will and how your assets are to be held to avoid probate, if that was one of your goals, and how you will reduce or minimize any estate taxes at death.

Any suggestion made should be understandable to you, and, certainly, any recommendations for a change should be thoroughly explained.

You have now been through the analysis part, the planning stage, and have arrived at the action or implementation stage.

If you accept your plan and understand it, you should be able to fight through the temptation to procrastinate that will start to fall over you. It can be very difficult to get started, especially when your plan calls for some major restructuring of how you have done things in the past.

I am sure many a plan has been simply filed away. This is probably one of the reasons that many planners are fee-only practitioners. That is, they will draw you a plan for a fee ranging between a couple of hundred dollars to $5,000 depending on the complexity of your situation and/or the amount of assets involved. Other planners earn their money by having you implement the plan through them so they can earn the commissions involved. Some have an arrangement that employs both fees and commissions. Each says their method is the fairest and best for the client. I am not ready to say one way is better than another, but you should know in advance how your planner will be making his or her money.

WHAT TO CONFIDE TO YOUR PLANNER

A lot of managing a person's finances, or at least designing a personal financial plan for them, is gathering the data.

But I do not mean just numbers. Oh sure, you need to know all of the sources of income and a list of expenditures. What the portfolio looks like, the tax bracket, etc. But every bit as important is gathering the personal data.

For example, what is your client's tolerance for risk?

If they have no experience with certain types of investments, will they position money there anyway because it is part of the plan or are they committed to just those things they are familiar with already?

If it is a couple, do they both really want all the assets to go to the surviving spouse at the death of the first or does one of them wish deep down they could control where it goes even after their death?

So you see in a way, depending on the amount of planning you expect from your planner, you really need to give as much information as you can. If you have selected the right person, they will use this information to design a plan that matches your wishes.

I know, when I am working with people for the first time, most of the first appointment seems to be used in gathering up their thoughts. That is not to say to make a simple buy or sell in the market you need to go through all this process. Or if all you need is to establish a living trust, that there is a need to get into a full review of your current situation. It would not hurt, but it is not necessary.

But if you are going in to see someone about your finances, you can make the session a lot more useful if you try to collect your thoughts ahead of time. You and your spouse, if you are married, should go over a list of items and try to come to some kind of agreement on what you really want.

Here is a sample of what to look at. Your list might look different.

What are your chief goals? What is most important to you right now? Is it finding ways to lower your taxes? Is it providing for your spouse after your death? Is it paying for your children's education?

What degree of risk can you and your spouse live with? So often I find one person is willing to make investments that makes the other person just cringe. That is not going to work. Because the spouse fearing the risk will never really feel comfortable with the investment, and it will become a future source of distress between you. Not to mention what you will go through if the investment ever turns sour.

How do you want to leave your estate when you die? What will be given to whom? Should it be given outright or should there be some qualifiers such as age, marital status and so forth?

Who would be a good guardian for your children if you die while they are still young? Do you have someone in mind to act as your personal representative to take care of matters after your death?

If you are still working, when would you like to retire and will your living style change very much?

Where do you think interest rates will be several years from now? What level of inflation do you expect to see throughout the next decade?

Have you been able to put together, at least in rough form, a list of all your income sources and your expenditures? Both fixed ones like the mortgage and variable ones like entertainment?

Knowing this kind of information allows a professional to analyze financial data through a screen to fashion a plan that has meaning for you. That's when it is personal financial planning.

SOME THINGS SHOULD NOT BE PUT OFF

Most people do not like going to see a doctor.

It may be because they are afraid they are going to be told something they really don't want to hear. Or maybe they just hate to take the time. They figure, if a little ailment comes up, they can solve it by getting a little more rest or taking some aspirin.

People put off seeing a financial planner for much the same reasons, even though numerous surveys show people believe planners are in the best position to help them with their overall financial concerns.

But just as when a major illness comes along, we make the effort to see the doctor; when a major financial event takes place, it should no longer be catch as catch can.

I am thinking, for example, of all these people who have lost their jobs because of layoffs or early retirement, at major companies such as Eastern Airlines, Pratt & Whitney and IBM. If there was ever a time a person should get his or her finances reviewed, this is it.

Just as when you visit the doctor, you may not like to hear what the results will be at a financial planner's office. Maybe you will be told to ease up on your outgoing cash flow and increase your savings, or else risk not being able to retire in the style you wanted. On the other hand, you may walk out with he peace of mind of knowing everything is running along smoothly. Either way, you owe it to yourself and your family to find out.

Because financial planning is still pretty much an unregulated business, you will probably find any number of people willing to "plan" your finances. So here are a few guidelines as to what you might expect or what to watch out for.

You will find qualified people to plan your finances at local brokerage offices and individual planning offices. Even some banks and savings and loans are getting into the planning business, as are some accountants.

All things being equal, if you have a choice, select a certified financial planner, registered financial planner, chartered financial consultant, certified life underwriter or the like. On the other hand, no certification is as important as integrity and knowledge. It's always a good idea to ask for references.

Some planners will charge you a fee for preparing your plan, while others might not. If the fee is not large, I recommend you go this route. That way you are under no obligation, real or imagined, to go back to that individual or firm. Of course, if you got along with the planner and believed he or she knew what they were doing, it would make the most sense to continue to work with him or her.

The plan you receive should be in writing. It should cover areas of concern in detail, not generalities.

For example, if you have not yet retired, your plan should look at when you want to retire and with how much money and then calculate how much you need to save between now and then to reach your goal.

The plan should also review your insurance needs and make sure you are not paying more than you need and that you have adequate coverage.

It should examine your income and expenditures.

It should tell you about the advantages of having a will and make sure the one you may already have is still doing what you need.

It should answer questions, such as whether a trust could benefit you and your heirs, what your family net worth looks like and whether your investment portfolio, if you have one, is designed to further your goals.

As you can see, you need more than the simple assets allocation plan that many people pass off as financial planning.

What could all this cost you? Some time, that is for sure, rounding up background information. And some dollars. But you will have peace of mind that you probably never had before and ideas that should more than pay for themselves.

SIMPLE THINGS A PLANNER MIGHT QUICKLY SPOT

With so much attention given these days to financial planning, it is no wonder we get a little confused over what it is, or even, what it can do for us.

There are probably a score of definitions, but the one I like best says financial planning is following a planned approach by which you maximize your assets to reach an objective you have set.

This definition implies a lot more than just buying a stock when it is low and selling it when it has climbed, or going from a certificate of deposit paying a low rate of return to a higher-yielding government security.

It means being aware of the many legal and tax aspects that are a part of most decisions we make today.

Here are a few samples of how this really works on a day-to-day basis.

Mrs. Johnson has been a client for a short time. She has about $300,000 of assets in her name alone. Her husband, it is learned, has been keeping, in his name, assets worth about the same amount. She walks in one day with him and announces she would like to purchase some common stock.

Purchasing the stock may or may not turn out to be a profitable move for Mrs. Johnson. However, if she is asked whether the security should be put into joint registration with her husband, so at the time of death the securities will pass to the other without any of the expense or delay of probate, she is already ahead.

Someone should explain to the Johnsons the significance of having their securities registered in separate names as opposed to being jointly held.

You might come across a situation in which the amount of assets owned by each spouse is very large. In this case, it is probably better for each spouse to own some of the assets in his or her own name and register them in a living trust.

A case in point: The husband wants to buy some bonds and asks that they be placed into a new account with his wife's name only. In a case like this, it is more important to know that these securities will go through probate unless they are put into a living trust than whether the bonds were purchased at a quarter of a point better or worse in price.

In other words, whether the markets go up or down may not mean as much in actual savings or accumulation as whether the securities are registered properly.

FINANCIAL PLANNING FOR THE YOUNG

So much of what you read and hear about estate and financial planning is directed to people over 55 years.

But, if you are one of the many two career couples with young children, should you too be concerned with planning your estate?

The answer is yes.

Granted, in all likelihood, your focus will not be so much on planning techniques to save on estate taxes as making sure your spouse can go on living in a style he or she is used to and that the children will be provided for, in the event both of you die at the same time.

Typically, the two-career family takes on raising children, buying a bigger house, nicer cars, all with the expectation they will always earn more money next year and no disaster will come their way.

And yet, you absolutely need to address the question of what would happen if one of you were to die. How would the other get along what with the mortgage, child-raising costs and so forth? The answer, of course, is having adequate insurance.

Consider the financial impact to a couple of either spouse dying suddenly. A half or a quarter of the pair's income is gone, and yet big capital expenses such as a home mortgage and the future education of the children remain.

If it is the wife who dies, chances are the husband's career may not move up as rapidly as he thought. Even if he pays for someone to perform many of the daily household chores, he would still not be able to devote as much time as he planned to his career while the children are so young.

If it is the husband who dies, the wife might wish there was enough money available to take care of the mortgage and other bills so she could stop working and concentrate on the children.

Couples need to realistically figure out what it would take to see that the surviving spouse could go on living the way they want and protect the family unit. You need to sit down with your financial planner or a trusted insurance agent to review what coverage you already have.

For example, most people will have some coverage through their place of employment. Or, perhaps they took out mortgage insurance. Only then can you determine the kind, the amount and the cost of buying the additional protection you need.

For young couples requiring a lot of protection and not having too much money available, term insurance is often the type to get. Try to have as flexible a policy as possible, even though all those options will increase the cost of the premium. For example, you might want the ability to convert the policy over to a whole life policy, or be able to get additional insurance even though your health has deteriorated.

The other major area often overlooked by new parents is what will happen to your children in the event you both suddenly die? Who will be responsible for their upbringing? Will there be any money left to help the person named to raise them?

Another problem to avoid:

If you do not specify a particular person, such as a brother or sister, the court might agree to have another family member living close by become the children's guardian. If you would not like to see this left to chance, you need to state in your will just who it is you would like to serve as your children's legal guardian.

And if you are like most people at this stage of your life, your estate is not too large and a will is all you really need to plan for the proper passing of your assets to a surviving spouse or to the children, should you both die at the same time.

That is not to say there might not be some non-tax reasons you will want to consider a trust in addition to a will. For example, two spouses agree the large estate that will be left in the event one of them dies prematurely should be used solely for the benefit of the children. Well, to make sure plans are not changed afterwards, the insurance proceeds could be placed in a trust so the surviving spouse could not squander them or lose them through a second marriage.

WIVES SHOULD BE INVOLVED

This part is going to be about two different women. But if you read closely, you will see that it is about many women.

The stories deal with premature death, divorce and small fortunes. What is common to each, at least the part we are going to look at, is the management of money. This is something basic to our welfare, and yet women historically have been discouraged from learning about handling money.

This is even more ironic, when you consider that women are most often the ones who suddenly, through divorce or death, find themselves thrown into the world without knowing the basic fundamentals of handling large sums of money.

Let us start with Betty. She is somewhat younger than her husband. They live comfortably. Suddenly her husband dies.

Betty, like many women, was brought up in a time when women were responsible for household activities and were not supposed to get involved with any of the money decisions. There was always money to purchase anything she wanted, and her husband always told her not to worry about finances.

While her husband may have thought he was being an excellent provider and protecting her from money worries, what he really did was isolate her — financially speaking.

A few weeks after his demise, Betty, getting over her initial shock of being left alone, has bills to pay and all kinds of financial statements and inquiries coming in the mailbox.

Betty is having to scramble to locate all of the bank accounts, brokerage accounts, insurance policies, car titles and on and on. She feels abandoned and swamped under.

At this stage, because a sizable estate is involved, many people are offering to help her. But Betty is experienced enough to know that, while some of these people may have her best interest at heart, they do not have the skill required to do the proper planning for her. Conversely, there are those that would seem to have the skills, but she cannot be sure they would have her best interest in mind.

With just a minimal amount of time, Betty could have been shown where all the legal documents are kept, where the different accounts are located and what things may need her attention first, should her husband die.

Her husband could have made sure Betty had the opportunity to meet with the professional people he had dealt with over the years and had come to trust. He could have told her to whom she could turn, to help her make the many financial decisions she now faces.

Let us call our second woman Sue. Her situation is becoming more and more common in America.

She had lived comfortably with her husband. He was successful financially, and she was often photographed at the proper social functions. However, at 50 years of age, she suddenly finds herself divorced. She has no real employment skills and, in disbelief, stares at a divorce settlement that she is supposed to live on for the rest of her years.

Like Betty, Sue had always trusted someone else to worry about money. Neither of these women had any experience in managing the nest egg.

Faced with the sudden burden of having to make major financial decisions, both of these women may be tempted to remarry just so they can escape the responsibilities of handling money.

Let us hope instead, they make a commitment to themselves to never again be so vulnerable. They need to read, study and attend seminars and classes on basic finances to familiarize themselves with money management. They will also need to find an adviser they can trust.

Some men attempt to keep their wives from being involved with financial matters because they themselves are not all that proficient at it, and they fear losing power to their wives. They might feel they have lost another one of their domains. After all, men are expected to be wizards at handling money.

On the positive side, I find more and more husbands and wives coming together to my seminars or financial interviews. But there are still too many women who do not want to face the fact they may live a large part of their lives without a husband/money manager. So men, if nothing else, introduce them to some of the people you are working with now and have come to respect and trust.

The last word, "Trust", opens up a whole new idea for another column. Would a trust left for the surviving spouse be the answer? There are those who think so. We can examine this idea later.

CHAPTER 7
CHARITABLE STRATEGIES

ADVANTAGES OF DONATING STOCK
FOR YOU AND CHARITY

"It is a far better thing to give than to receive."

I do not know who said that originally, but it only stands to reason. First of all, you have to have before you can give, so that means you are doing well, and secondly, giving makes you feel good.

But let us not kid ourselves. Most big gift giving is done with the anticipation of a little tax savings as well. If you doubt that, think how hard the charities fought a couple of years ago to defeat the section of the treasury tax proposals that would limit the amount you would be able to save on your taxes with your gift. They knew how important it was to keep gift giving attached to tax savings.

And, if you are thinking of making a charitable gift, consider this: If giving cash is wonderful, giving appreciated assets can be even more meaningful.

Why?

Let's say, you are considering making a sizable contribution of $50,000 to your favorite charity. If you write out a check for that amount, you will no longer have the interest earning power from those dollars.

On the other hand, let us say you have some shares

of a security in your portfolio you purchased quite some time ago when you were concentrating more on growth than income.

For example, you purchased a stock at $20 a share that went to $65. Like a lot of growth stocks, it pays little in dividends. You are in a high tax bracket, and you would prefer to have this money working for you in tax-free municipals or a real estate partnership, giving you quarterly checks sheltered from taxes. But heavens, you are not about to sell the stock and take that whopping capital gain.

To feel this way is quite normal. But here is where you and your charity can team up to your joint benefit.

Under current tax law, you can give the charity say, 1,000 shares of this stock. The charity accepts your gift and records it as a gift at its present market value. For our example, $65 times 1,000 shares or a $65,000 gift.

Under current law, you can take the $65,000 as a tax deduction on your income tax. Because it was long-term securities you gave, you can take off an amount equal to 30 percent of your adjusted gross income. If you had an adjusted gross income of $100,000, it would mean you could take a deduction up to $30,000.

What about the other $35,000 I said you could deduct?

The law says you can carry forward any unused part of the deduction for as many as five years until you use it up. So, next year you would have another deduction.

Now, the charity might decide to sell the securities you gave it right away. No problem. Neither the charity nor you will have to pay any tax on the appreciation. See how you both benefit?

If you had sold this stock first, you would have had less money to give to charity because of the taxes you would have have had to pay on the gain. You end up making a gift of more value than you might have been able to otherwise and the charity gets more money to carry out its work.

By the way, if you have securities with a loss in them, you would be better off selling the securities yourself and taking the loss against your other gains or against your ordinary income and giving the proceeds to the charity.

This is just one simple idea of gift giving that can benefit you. Some are a little more complicated, such as setting up a charitable trust that will give you income now and still allow you to claim a tax deduction.

THIS CHARITABLE TRUST DOUBLES AS A TAX SHELTER

Let us say you find yourself in one of these situations:

A) You own some raw land or common stocks that have greatly appreciated. You could use more income from these assets but hesitate to sell them because of the capital gain that will occur.

B) You find yourself in a high tax bracket now and could use some tax sheltering, but before too long you will be in a lower bracket and will need more income.

C) You are in a high tax bracket, and your income needs sheltering. You also are trying to help your parents financially.

In each of these cases and with others like them, the solution to your problem could be something called a charitable remainder unitrust.

Basically, this is a legal vehicle that will allow the individual setting it up to get a tax write-off for making a gift to a charity and also allow that person, or whomever he or she designates, to receive income from the assets for the rest of his or her life, with the remainder amount going to the charity.

You also benefit by knowing you are helping a favorite charity, and in cases where you may be concerned about your surviving spouse being able to manage funds on their own, you arrange to have that task done for him or her.

Like most trust vehicles, you can have your attorney draw the plan in a way that will have the greatest benefit for you.

For example, Mr. and Mrs. Carson are both in their late 60's. At this stage of their lives, they could use some additional income from their assets. Unfortunately, a great deal of their portfolio is in two growth stocks that Mr. Carson acquired years ago. He would like to sell these stocks and put the money into a government fund, or some other high-yielding investment, but his cost basis is so low he hesitates to sell the securities and pay such a large amount out for taxes.

The Carsons could establish a charitable remainder unitrust naming a church, college, hospital or other recognized charitable institution as the ultimate beneficiary. The Carsons then would transfer the two securities to the trust, keeping the low-cost basis. The charity would accept them and sell the issues if so desired. Neither the Carsons nor the charity would have to pay taxes on the appreciation that was realized.

The Carsons would be able to claim a tax deduction for the value of the gifts at today's fair market value, thereby maximizing their gift.

The trust is instructed by the Carsons to pay out a yearly income of a certain percentage of the trust assets for the rest of their lives.

For example, if the trust they established had $50,000, and they asked for 10 percent, they would get $5,000. If the following year the trust grew to $55,000, they would receive $5,500.

Look at our second situation. You could set up the trust

and ask for the same 10-percent income. But by setting up the trust in growth items that will not generate enough income to pay you that 10 percent, you can have the money owed to you and paid later on. After a dozen years or so, you will be in a lower tax bracket. The trust switches the assets to higher yielding ones and pays you your required income stream, plus what it owed you from before.

In our third scenario, when the trust is established, the income is directed to go to your parents rather than yourself. You still get the charitable tax deduction.

One thing you cannot do is change your mind after you have funded the trust. The law requires it to be an irrevocable trust. But if you have a situation along these lines, you should discuss the merits of this idea with your financial advisor and a lawyer experienced in trusts.

CHARITABLE TRUSTS THAT HELP YOU AND LOVED ONES

"Killing two birds with one stone" has always been one of those old-time sayings I really like.

How would you like to be able to: 1) give some securities or other capital asset such as a parcel of land, to a charity, such as a hospital, or your alma mater or church, and get a tax deduction; 2) have that charity pay you income for the rest of your life; and 3) at the same time reduce the size of your taxable estate?

Sounds interesting?

Well, the law allows you to do all this by establishing an irrevocable charitable remainder trust, funding it with highly appreciated assets and then instructing the charity to pay you or whomever you select, a certain percentage of income.

Okay, let us take that paragraph apart so we can

more readily understand what is involved and then look at an example.

Irrevocable means you are giving away the assets you put into the trust forever. That is how you are reducing the size of your estate. At your death the assets you transferred to the charitable trust are not under your control so no estate taxes will have to be paid on them.

Charitable means, as you would think, a bona fide charity.

Remainder trust means, after the death of the person or persons receiving income from the trust, the remaining assets belong to the charity.

Why do I say these kinds of trusts should be funded with highly appreciated assets?

Let us take the case of an elderly widow. She and her husband have owned a portfolio of blue-chip securities for 40 years. He recently died leaving everything to her. She needs or would like some additional income. However, all of the securities in the portfolio are growth-oriented stocks that pay little or no dividends.

You might say sell them and buy higher yielding investments. And that is what is commonly done. But in this case, the stocks have such a low-cost basis, taxes would eat up most of her principal. And it so happens that she has no other family and is considering leaving anything she has left at her demise to charity.

Using an irrevocable charitable remainder trust, she transfers the assets into the trust and instructs the charity to pay her a certain percent of income for the rest of her life.

The charity would probably sell the assets given it, pay no capital gains, and therefore have all the market value of the securities to invest. That way the trust can easily deliver to her the 10 percent or so income she requested.

Our widow would also receive a nice charitable tax

deduction for making the gift, and she would have the satisfaction of living to see her contribution help the charity.

The amount of the charitable tax deduction is figured by using a formula involving the age of the giver, the percent of income asked for, and of course, the amount of assets being transferred.

This area of planning has many, many variations to it. Here is an example of another creative use for it.

How about a sports star who is making a really big income now, but, after retirement, will probably be looking for additional income?

He could set up the trust and fund it with cash, taking a substantial charitable tax deduction at the same time. Only, in this case, the charity is instructed that in any years the trust does not earn enough income to pay the athlete his percentage, that amount has to be made up at a later date.

The charity then cooperates by investing his assets into vehicles that have a lot of growth potential but little income. Therefore, for years he receives little income and the amount owed him builds up. Finally, when he retires from the game and would like to add to his income, the charity revises the portfolio to produce a lot of income and pays him large annual amounts to make up for the past payments missed.

CHARITABLE DONATIONS THAT PAY "YOU" AT INCOME TAX TIME

Christmas 'tis the season to be jolly — and charitable.

Motivated by the spirit of the holiday season, December is one of the most profitable months for charities. Filled with the spirit of good will to all, Americans are a much easier touch for donations during the holidays, than say, right after paying their income taxes.

And that is probably the other reason December is such a popular gift giving time.

Many people have discovered they can make donations to their favorite charity and take a tax deduction in the process. Charities are often giving seminars showing people how they can do this effectively.

So let us take a moment and cover the basic guidelines. There have been some changes since the Tax Reform Act of 1986.

The law says that a deduction must be made to an organization recognized as a proper charity by the Treasury Department. The most familiar are churches, schools and hospitals.

The second group of charities are classified as private foundations. If you are unsure to which class a charity belongs, you can always look it up in a publication put out by the superintendent of documents in Washington, D.C. Is there anything they do not publish a booklet on?

To avoid confusion, let us confine ourselves to the first classification of charitable organizations.

The law says that, when you make a contribution of cash or a security held short-term, you can claim a deduction for what it cost you. Note, not its fair market value, but what it cost you. You can deduct an amount up to half of what your adjusted gross income is for the year. If your contribution is more than that, you are able to carry the balance forward to be used over the next five years.

For example, you have an adjusted gross income of $45,000. You make a gift of $40,000 in cash. In the year you make the gift, you can deduct only $22,500.

Now, let us take the case of making a gift with an asset held long term.

In this case, the government says you can claim the fair market value of the stock, bonds or ranch as the amount of the deduction — not what you paid for them. But in this case, you can only take the deduction against 30 percent of your adjusted gross income, not 50 percent as it was with cash and short-term assets.

And this is very important: In all cases, the gift must be made without any strings attached. As the French say, fait accompli.

The gift must also be made in the year you want to claim the deduction. In other words, you cannot be making a promise of a gift next year, or at your death, to get the deduction now. A pledge does not count in the eyes of the IRS.

And if you are contemplating giving an appreciated security, the IRS has some rules you need to follow so you can claim the deduction at the time you plan to claim it.

You cannot just decide on December 31 that you are going to give some stock to a charity and work the details out later. The gift must be made. To follow the rules, you should consult your accountant as far ahead of time as possible for guidance.

Generally, you will find that if you are mailing a certificate that is signed by you, the date you mailed it to the charity will be acceptable in terms of an IRS claim. If you are sending the certificate to a transfer agent to transfer it from your name to the name of the charity, the gift will not be recognized until the agent has made the change on their books. Notice, this is not the date you sent the agent the certificate.

In the common case where your securities are being held by a brokerage house in street name, you can speed up the transfer by having the charity appoint your broker as its agent and have the broker acknowledge, in writing, he or she is acting as agent for the charity in this transfer. In this case, a charitable transfer can be done almost instantly, all at your broker's office.

CHAPTER 8
BUYING INSURANCE

USING INSURANCE TO BIND TOP EXECUTIVES

Sometimes, it is the rather simple things that are overlooked when it comes to planning, whether it is doing little projects around the house or planning your personal finances.

I wonder, for example, how many small to medium-size businesses with one or two key executives have considered providing a meaningful economic benefit such as extra life insurance as an added incentive to keep these important people.

It would be difficult to find any working executive today who would say that he or she has enough insurance coverage. Caught between the squeeze of higher education costs, bigger mortgages and maintaining a demanding social schedule, many people have let their insurance coverage be dictated by whatever the company provides.

These people are gambling they will not die unexpectedly, because in many cases, their existing insurance coverage would not allow their families to go on living in their current lifestyle. Depending on the size of the family and everyone's ages, chances are, without immediate careful financial planning, inflation would take over the family's resources in a rather short time.

Business owners, who do not want to lose a key executive, should try a little creative planning of their own and give extra life insurance as an earnings supplement to the employee. Both the employer and the employee should come out ahead.

For the employee, there will be extra insurance coverage for the family so that no sudden tragedy will leave the spouse and the children financially devastated. While it is true the annual premiums paid by the employer for the policy will count as taxable ordinary income for the employee, the employee is getting a policy much more cheaply than if he or she bought it with after tax dollars.

If permanent cash value life insurance is bought, it will have all the tax advantages of any other life insurance policy. This means, for example, the insurance proceeds paid at death are going income-tax free to the beneficiaries. However, remember the value of the policy will be included in the estate of the executive recorded as owner, so that executive should be sure to have his or her overall finances reviewed in order to avoid any unnecessary estate taxes.

The owner of the policy also benefits from the cash value of the policy which accumulates free of current income taxes. If you select one of the newer styled policies, the interest rate earned on the cash values will be closer to reality. And this extra savings can be a real source of supplemental retirement benefits.

For the employer, of course, the premiums paid will be tax deductible as a business expense. With a permanent cash value policy, the premiums can be level and fixed, which will make payments easier to plan. It is also easy to administer this benefit because it requires no government approval, or forms to be filled out.

Employers should also like the fact that because these are unqualified dollars, they can select which employees will get this bonus. So it is a benefit with a great deal of flexibility.

If you are a business owner and this sounds like something you would like to look into, you should contact your insurance agent or financial planner to see how much this would cost you. An expert will help you select the proper insurance policy and set it up to maximize the benefits to everyone.

If you are an executive employee reading this and you believe it would be a good incentive for you and perhaps a few others at your company, why not send a copy of this article to the head officer with a little note saying this looks like a good idea.

DISABILITY CAN THREATEN YOUR FUTURE

Whenever I talk to people about planning their finances, one of the areas I discuss is adequate insurance coverage.

What good is a super financial plan if it does not provide for emergencies such as death of the major breadwinner?

Perhaps even financially worse, the major wage-earner could suffer some mental or physical disability that would make him or her unable to bring in money for months. Such a major illness, followed by a long period of convalescence, can completely wipe out anyone's savings and leave a family in financial ruin.

While social security provides some kind of safety net, how much a disabled person receives depends a great deal on how much he or she has paid into the program. Additionally, the government might not view your particular disability as a disability. Social Security might decide while you cannot return to your regular line of work with your illness, you should look for some other kind of job.

If the disability is caused by an accident at work, a person could be in line for some benefit through workman's compensation. You should check to see just how much coverage you might receive, how soon it will start following a disability and whether the amount received will be reduced if you receive benefits from other sources, such as social security.

If you determine you definitely would have a problem if all at once you were to suffer a long-term disability due to illness or accident, you should try to estimate just how much the shortfall will be on a monthly or annual basis. You will need to have an insurance policy pick up the difference.

Bear in mind, if your annual salary is, for example, $50,000, you actually take home less than that. Work with the after-tax amount. The disability payments you receive from your insurance policy will be free from taxes.

To figure out what you will need to meet expenses with this income gone, start with your expense figure and subtract the amount you would be entitled to from social security. The average benefit for a single person is about $500, and $900 for someone with dependents. Also subtract any amount your spouse is currently bringing in or might be able to if he or she worked outside the home. Figure any investment income you might be receiving.

The amount you are still short would be the amount a good disability insurance policy could cover.

For example:

    Current monthly expenses $3,600

Less

    Income from social security 900
    Income from investments 250

Income from spouse
   part-time employment 450
Equals shortfall
   Amount needed from insurance ... $2,000

Be sure you select an insurance representative who fully understands this particular area of insurance and is able to fully explain the kind of coverage you are buying. You want to make sure that:

   — Your benefits will not be reduced by other coverage.

   — The policy will have a liberal interpretation of what constitutes disability. You do not want to be laid up in bed before the policy will pay.

   — The policy is non-cancelable and guaranteed renewable.

   — Your premiums will be waived a relatively short time after a claim has been made.

   — Disability from any cause, whether job related or not, will be covered.

   — The payments you receive will be adjusted for inflation.

INSURANCE YOU USE
WHILE YOU ARE ALIVE

One of the good planning ideas attendees came away with from our big two-day seminar on running a small business was how crucial it was to have disability insurance on yourself.

It is more common for people to think only in terms of life insurance to protect their families should they die suddenly. They tend to forget that they need to protect their ability to earn a living because that is what is going to continue to provide their lifestyle.

How real of a threat is a temporary disability?

According to statistics revealed by the commissioner's disability tables, three out of 10 Americans will become disabled for three months or more between the ages of 35 and 65.

It is interesting that the majority of these disabilities are illness related.

I suppose this is a result of better on-the-job safety procedures and better medical techniques. For example, today a victim of a heart attack has a greater chance of surviving although there will usually be a convalescence period.

To find out whether your family could survive your suffering a major disability, you should sit down and figure out all your monthly expenses. Things like rent or mortgage, car payments, food and clothing, electric and telephone and so forth.

Then look at what sources you have available to draw upon. This list will include savings, assets that can be easily sold, perhaps a group disability policy you have at work or money available from family members.

If you are coming up short, you should face the fact that you need to look into buying a policy to make up the difference.

There are many policies out there, so let me give you the specific policy features you need to be aware of and either you or your financial advisor should use to compare policies.

Decide how long you can go without your payroll or insurance check coming in.

The reason for this is the longer you can delay the

start-up of the insurance payment, the cheaper the insurance policy will be. Try to arrange your finances so you can cover the first three months on your own. The savings are dramatic.

Be sure your policy is guaranteed renewable and noncancelable. You do not want to have the threat of being cut off by the insurance company once you start to collect, and you certainly do not want to face increased premiums.

Find out how large a payment they will make and decide how long you want the coverage. For example, if you have annual income of $50,000 a year, normally the most coverage they will allow you to buy is about 60 to 80 percent of that amount. They want you to have an incentive to get back to work.

You may elect to have the coverage for only a year to save some premium costs, but you would be wise to keep the coverage at least to age 65, even if it means stretching out the time period before payments start to keep policy costs down.

One of the most important differences to analyze is the company's definition of disabled.

It is less expensive to buy a policy that says you are disabled only when you cannot find work similar to your original occupation. These can be interpreted to mean a trial lawyer who loses his or her voice will not be considered disabled if they can do legal research for other attorneys.

It is much more expensive to have an "own occupation" definition of disability, but if you are a skilled professional, this will be a feature worth including.

There are some other features you can consider, all at extra cost, but these are certainly the key ones to go after in any policy you decide to buy.

HOW TO PLAN FOR SHORT TERM RISKS

Financial planners often refer to insurance as "risk reduction".

And it is not just because the word insurance has about as much charisma as dental plaque.

It is because insurance is indeed a way to reduce risk to our financial well-being.

Sometimes after we have analyzed a situation, we determine there is little we can do to avoid a risk. Like driving an automobile to work every day. Or keeping our home from burning down. We look to insurance to transfer that damage exposure to someone else.

However, we are not always careful to cover all the risks. Perhaps, like taxes, risk is just something we would prefer not to deal with, so we ignore it.

Here is an example.

A young couple, with two children, call them yuppies if you like, appear to have everything going very smoothly. He is the principal wage-earner and is covered with life insurance through his company. He has also accumulated several smaller policies along the way.

The need for this insurance is obvious. If the husband dies, his surviving spouse will need a lot of money to carry on the raising of the two children, paying the mortgage and so forth. This man's sudden death and loss of income would be a tragedy to the family.

But, do you know what could be even worse financially?

What if the husband came down with a crippling illness or he suffered an accident that did not take his life, but disabled him so he could not work? Even if he could find work, it would probably not come near to matching his old income.

Now, not only does this family have the problem of

lost income, but chances are there would be increased expenses as well because of the husband's illness or injury. It would be a double blow.

Fortunately, many of us are covered for situations like this either by insurance plans at our place of employment or through social security. That may be all the coverage you need. But, then again, it may not.

That is why you should take a good long look at your finances to see whether you need to have your own disability insurance coverage.

If you are covered by your employer, find out just how much you will be paid if you should have to go on disability. Ask whether that amount is reduced if and when social security starts making payments. It can vary.

You should find out how long you would have to be off your job before you would start collecting insurance. It is not uncommon for there to be a three-month or longer waiting period. Now all the financial planning rules say you should have at least three months income stashed in a money market fund. But if you are like a lot of people, you may not.

What happens when it comes time to make the mortgage payment and the car loan or cover the telephone and electric bills?

If you do not know when you will ever have that much savings built up, you might ask your insurance agent about a short-term disability plan that could get you over the hurdle until your other insurance or benefits take effect.

If your only coverage for disability is going to come from social security, you really might need one of those short-term policies. Social security makes you wait five months before giving you a check.

If you do decide to look into a disability insurance policy, be sure to compare. Pay particular attention to how the insurance company defines disability. Obviously, you would like a policy that gives a broad definition, not one that says as long as you can find any kind of work, you are not disabled.

Because you probably will never sit down yourself and look over all your different policies, you should find an insurance agent or financial planner you trust in order to get some guidance. Call and ask for an appointment to review your disability coverage. Then you will find out just how well you are covered.

CHAPTER 9
RETIREMENT PLANNING

CAN YOU AFFORD TO LIVE ON GOLDEN POND?

When I did my big Money Matters seminar called PLANNING FOR THE LATTER YEARS — LIVING IT OUT ON GOLDEN POND, one of the topics of greatest interest was health care.

It was no surprise. As reported in *Business Week*, the number of Americans over 65 today is 28.6 million, and the number is expected to reach 35 million by the year 2000. By some estimates, one out of four of this group needs long-term care.

Those over 85 — where three out of five require long-term care — number 2.7 million today and are projected to number five million by the year 2000.

With figures that high, chances are right now you know someone who requires some sort of nursing home care. And with our increasing life span, while we may not like to think of ever having to spend time in a nursing home, the percentages are getting pretty high that we could.

Could you or your family afford a prolonged stay at a convalescent home? Studies show that care will run $22,000 to $40,000 per year.

When you consider the average person stays in such a

nursing home for approximately two years, you can see why the Department of Health and Human Services says nursing home care is the number one health-care expense for older adults.

An extended stay can be devastating.

In fact, when I plan for older clients, I try to be sure they understand that one of the real threats to their financial peace of mind is a long-term illness or disability.

In our younger working years, we protect against this threat to our families by carrying disability insurance. But after retirement, we have to continue to protect against this.

In conversations, I find many people have a vague idea that Medicare or Medicaid will cover any stay at a nursing home. This is more wishful thinking.

Medicare only applies to cases involving what is termed skilled nursing care and will pay partial eligible expenses for eight days followed by full payments through the 150th day.

However, the majority of extended convalescent care is not skilled nursing care, where a person requires attention prescribed by a doctor and administered by a skilled nurse, but rather for what is classed as intermediate care or custodial care. Intermediate care may require a nurse, but in general it is helping with routine activities such as getting out of bed, bathing and eating.

Studies show that very few people need skilled extended care for long periods. For example, a person suffering loss of motor functions as a result of suffering a stroke, will often need months of custodial care but little of what could be termed skilled care.

While it is true that Medicaid will cover all areas of convalescence, whether it is skilled or custodial or intermediate care, the coverage is only for those that can be classed as poor.

Medicaid is a state-assistance program, and each state has its own definition of poor. Basically, they all take the position that you must have first gone through your savings and income before the state will contribute.

In Florida, for example, the state looks for a person's income to be no higher than about $10,000 and for the person to have access to virtually no other resources.

If the person facing convalescence is married, the state looks at all of the income and resources belonging to each spouse individually and jointly.

Even if Medicaid does start to pay, should the disabled spouse die first, the surviving spouse is left alone and with little or no assets to live the remaining years of his or her life.

Not a nice picture, is it?

We will discuss some ways you can protect your family from this catastrophe.

FIGURING OUT HOW MUCH YOU WILL NEED AT RETIREMENT

Financial planning for most people includes putting aside funds for when it comes time to retire.

Usually, it means holding back on spending now so there will be some dollars left to invest. And, in today's consumption-oriented society, no one wants to save any more than they have to.

For many reasons, it is difficult to project just how much money you will need at retirement time.

However, tables have been designed to at least give you some kind of idea what you should have accumulated by retirement. Try them out. I think you may get a real surprise.

The first table is designed to figure what you will need

at your first year of retirement, based on today's dollars. For example, you are 55 years old, earn $1,800 a month, and plan to retire at 65. That is 10 years until retirement; go down to 10 years and across to find an "accumulation factor" of 1.8.

TABLE 1

(based upon a 6% annual inflatin rate)

Years to Retirement	Accumulation Factor
5	1.4
10	1.8
15	2.4
20	3.2
25	4.3
30	5.7

This means that, even with certain expenses being eliminated, you would need $1,800 times 1.8 — $3,240 per month. For a year, it would be $38,880.

Naturally, if inflation stayed lower, you would need less. However, six percent is a reasonable projection.

The next step is to try to predict how much capital you will need to support yourself for your remaining retirement years. In other words, are you in danger of outliving your retirement nest egg?

In this case, we go to a table, assuming again a constant six-percent inflation rate. The table offers you several choices of investment rates of return. That is, after inflation and after taxes. You can choose what you think will be the most accurate rate of return on your retirement savings.

TABLE 2

Retirement Age — Rate of Return After 6% Inflation and After Taxes

	5%	6%	7%	8%	9%	10%
50	29.0	25.5	22.6	20.1	18.0	16.2
55	24.1	21.7	19.5	17.7	16.1	14.6
60	20.0	18.2	16.7	15.3	14.1	13.0
65	16.2	15.0	13.9	13.0	12.1	11.3
70	12.9	12.1	11.4	10.7	10.1	9.6

Go to the column on the left to find the age at which you expect to retire and then go across to the column that has the interest rate you expect and find that figure. For example, we said if you expected to retire at 65 and you think a real rate of return on your retirement funds will be 7 percent, the figure will be 13.9 percent.

Multiply that figure by what we first calculated to be an annual amount of $38,880 and you have $540,432. That would be the amount you would need at retirement.

If you come up with a figure that seems overwhelming, lest you despair, remember, you probably will have social security and a pension or other retirement plan throwing income your way. But it does mean you probably should be planning a little better for retirement.

YOUR OPTIONS, IF YOUR PLAN IS CANCELED

I have said previously that Congress did this country a disservice when it altered the rules on individual retirement savings plans.

I predicted, without the incentive of tax savings,

Americans would lose interest in funding IRAs and that would mean less savings overall in a country that needs to learn how to save. Sure enough, the major financial institutions did not mount, as they had in previous years, their blitzkrieg advertising campaigns to encourage everyone to put aside another $2,000 for retirement.

Further proof of the tax law's effect is being felt across the country as some of the nation's premier growth companies have decided to shut down some of their retirement assistance plans because of the Tax Reform Act of 1986.

Because I am sure this is going to happen to many others, it is a good time to review what a person's options are when a retirement plan terminates like this.

Again, like many things in finances, with everyone throwing things at you to look at and sign, it may seem more complicated than it is.

If the dollars in the retirement plan were put there before any taxes were taken out of them, then they are referred to as pre-tax dollars. This means you will have to include the amount as ordinary income and pay income taxes in the year you get the money.

In addition to paying regular taxes on the amount, you will pay an additional tax penalty of 10 percent on the amount you receive if you are younger than 59 1/2. There are a couple of exceptions to this, such as if you are at least 55 and already retired, or if you are disabled.

If you are like most people, you will decide to roll your money into an IRA roll-over plan. It can be done by having the dollars go directly from one company to another, or you can ask to receive your money and take as long as 60 days to put it into a roll-over plan yourself.

If you do decide to take the latter route, you should instruct the institution or company handling the plan you are leaving to not withhold any money for federal taxes.

Okay. You have decided to put off paying taxes on this

money until later in retirement. You now have to decide where you want this money to be working for you for the next five, 10 or 30 years.

If the amount of money is small, say, a couple thousand dollars, probably the simplest and least expensive idea is to try to choose an individual investment. It might be a bank certificate of deposit or a mutual fund company offering a family of funds. For most people with a smaller amount to roll-over, something like this makes the most sense to me.

However, those who are rolling over a larger amount, or perhaps have other smaller IRAs scattered around that can be combined into one IRA, I think you should take a look at one of the self-directed plans offered by all brokerage firms and some banks.

A self-directed plan allows you to invest your retirement dollars in the widest range of investments. This allows you the potential for better diversification and repositioning of your assets as you grow older and your needs change.

Besides having the certificates of deposit and mutual funds the simple plans offer, a self-directed plan offers everything from aggressive small-growth companies to zero-coupon treasury bonds.

You can diversify by spreading your money among annuities, government bonds, GNMAs, real estate, hundreds of different mutual fund families, even gold coins.

A self-directed plan also will usually allow you to deposit shares of stock you receive from an employee stock ownership plan.

While the simple plans usually costs less than $10 to establish, the self-directed plans will typically cost $25 or more to set up. That is why I say, if you have only a few dollars, you really are probably better off to stick with the investment plan.

Whenever you can, it is always a good idea to go, with your spouse if you are married, and discuss all your alternatives with a professional advisor.

TAX REFORM CHANGES
IRA WITHDRAWAL RULES

If you are currently withdrawing money from your Individual Retirement Account, or are about to start, you might be very interested in one of the changes brought about by one of the many new tax reform bills.

While many people put money aside in their IRA to help them get through retirement, there are those reaching retirement with such an asset base that they really do not need their IRA funds.

These people have probably been in a high tax bracket most of their working lives. The IRA funds they pull out will be taxed as ordinary income, and if a person is still in a high tax bracket, you can understand why he or she would just as soon not touch their IRA accounts.

While there is no change in the part of the law that says you can start taking out your IRA dollars at age 59 1/2 without any penalty for early withdrawal, or that you must start withdrawing from your IRA the year you turn 70 1/2, there is a change in how those withdrawals have to be made.

Prior to the change in the tax law, you had to take out an amount of money equal to a fraction of your life expectancy when you hit 70 1/2. To put it another way, the year you hit 70 1/2, they look up your life expectancy in the actuary tables and tell you that you have a life expectancy of so many years.

For example, a single woman turning 70 1/2 would probably be told she has a life expectancy of 15 years. So she would have to withdraw at least one-fifteenth of her IRA for that year. The following year, she would have to take out one-fourteenth of her IRA, and so forth. By the end of her 85th birthday, all of the money would be gone.

The new rule starts out the same.

However, the second year, instead of taking the one-fourteenth such as in the example, you would be able to again go to the tables and figure your life expectancy and take one fraction of those years.

It may not seem like a big deal, but according to the charts I have seen, it means a single woman who had depleted her IRA money by age 85 under the old rule would, under the new method, still have $107,000 in her IRA, having started with $100,000 when she was 70.

For someone not needing these funds and preferring to pass them on to others at death, this is a very significant factor.

Now, just to clear up a few other points before we give you some other comparisons between the old and the new rule:

If you start taking your IRA dollars out under the one fractions-at-a-time guidelines, should things change and you wish to take out more — or even all of it — in any given year, you are free to do so. You are not committed to maintaining the schedule once you start it, except that you must take out at least that amount.

If you are married when it comes time to start your yearly calculation, you can consider hooking up with your spouse and use a joint life expectancy if that will allow you to take out less. This would be particularly advantageous when a man has reached 70 1/2 and his wife is only 65. The woman has a longer life expectancy, and because the wife is younger in the first place, the couple's joint life expectancy would be much longer.

Now, here are some other examples showing the significant differences between the two methods.

For all of the examples, let us use a single male, age 70, starting with an IRA worth $100,000 that is earning a continued interest rate of 10 percent.

OLD LAW

Age	Withdrawal	Balance
70	$ 8,264	$101,736
73	11,302	101,828
76	13,434	91,482
80	21,376	51,517
83	6,749	0

NEW LAW

Age	Withdrawal	Balance
70	$ 8,264	$101,736
73	9,912	104,572
76	11,455	103,208
80	12,903	93,549
83	13,541	80,299

PUTTING YOUR IRA DOLLARS TO WORK

It is interesting how different people view their IRAs. Some see it as an opportunity to put $2,000 away and get a tax deduction for it. Others see it as their best hope for a better retirement.

Ideally, for those that still qualify for the tax deduction, it can be both.

But, too often people fall down on the job when it

comes to making sure they take full advantage of this retirement savings idea. They deduct the $2,000 and then just stick it somewhere. They fail to make sure the money is working hard enough. IRAs are different; what will be there when you go looking for yours at retirement could be vastly different from someone else's.

You see, what will be there depends on how you invest the money you put aside now. And with the self-directed style of IRA, you can put your dollars into everything from money market funds to commodities, from certificates of deposit to real estate or from zero-coupon treasuries to all kinds of mutual funds.

What you decide to do with your dollars should be a result of several factors.

For example, let us say you are only about five years from starting to pull out dollars from your retirement plan.

There would hardly be enough time to invest in a real estate limited partnership. They usually take about seven to 10 years to run full course. So, while real estate is by far and away one of the safest and best ways to make sure your IRA dollars are going to provide the purchasing power you will need when you go looking for those dollars at retirement, you may not have the time for this longer term investment.

Another factor you have to consider when choosing how you wish to invest your retirement money is how crucial the money will be to you when it comes time to retire.

Let us say you work in a job that does not have a retirement plan. You sense you will need every cent you are putting away into your IRA when it comes time to retire.

It would be nice to argue that you are exactly the person that needs to reach out and be a little more aggressive with your retirement dollars so there will be an account of some size to help you when you retire. You must understand and appreciate, however, the bigger the reward, the bigger the risk. Many best ideas have turned sour. When there is no tomorrow to make up the money lost, it seems to me to be hard to justify much risk.

You can turn to things like a money market fund. It will earn, at times, a relatively low yield. But at least you will know that, whether rates go up or down, your invested dollars will always be there. Whether you choose a bank, insurance company, mutual fund company or brokerage firm to put your dollars aside, there is little or no cost to maintain this kind of account.

A lot of people like zero-coupon treasuries. This investment permits you to lock up a given rate of return for a certain number of years, so you have a sure thing.

The zero-coupon security can be for a few years or out beyond the turn of the century. In general, the further out you go, the higher the rate of return you will be able to lock up.

I am always worried, though, at what we will think of these rates 15 and 20 years from now. People holding a corporate bond purchased 20 years ago yielding 3 1/2 percent are going to get all their principal back at maturity, but what a loss of opportunity to have sat there all that time at 3 1/2 percent. So be careful about locking up today's rate for more than about 10 to 12 years.

For those who want to be relatively safe but are worried about interest rates moving in the future, you can consider putting your money into a fixed deferred annuity.

Although people will ask, why should they put an investment that shelters taxes into a plan that shelters everything from taxes, the answer is, the deferred annuity tends to pay more than money market funds, and you can buy one that will adjust its interest rate on a yearly basis. That way your money will not be left behind if rates should climb.

Or you could invest in a government mutual fund. While there can be some fluctuation of your principal, the funds normally yield several percentages higher than a money market fund. If you reinvest your interest earned into additional shares, you should have less fluctuation of principal than what individual bond or unit trust holders might experience.

Slightly more aggressive, but certainly prudent are good quality growth funds. Most economists and analysts believe the country is in for basically good growth for the next number of years, and this would be one way to participate in that growth. Again, your shares will go up and down with the market, but good growth funds have a track record of doing well for the investor who reinvests his or her earnings and is patient.

Skipping over still several other choices you have, for the investor really wanting to put his or her IRA on a fast track — one way or the other — there is commodity investing. You can get in with a minimum of $2,000.

Remember, your $2,000 is going into an investment. Take a moment to match it with your financial needs and temperament. Whenever possible, spread your retirement dollars into several different kinds of investment ideas. You will increase your chances for a better retirement.

TRY THIS IRA SUBSTITUTE FOR SAVING

Here are some figures that should put more than a little fear into many.

Apparently 92 percent of Americans are on course to retiring with income of less than $25,000 per year. And that amount, according to the research, is from all available sources including social security, pension, savings and other investments.

As sad as that is, I think the problem has worsened since Congress has effectively dampened the attraction of IRA, probably the widest used savings plan this country ever saw since the war years — for a majority of workers.

So unless you have worked out a plan to ensure you will retire with enough assets to support your latter years in comfort, you need to realize you could end up in that 92 percent category.

One way out of the trap is to decide to keep putting a couple of thousand of dollars away each year into an idea that is pretty close to the standard IRA.

Again, to get the tax advantage of having all your dollars deposited accumulate with taxes deferred, we will have to turn to the insurance industry. If you recall, this is where we got the tax deferred annuity and the single premium life plan. So, because of the insurance being involved, maybe we can call this some sort of an insured retirement account and keep the same acronym IRA.

Here is how it works and why it could be a real boost to your retirement plans.

You open an account with any company handling the product. Right now that will more than likely be an insurance company or a brokerage firm. You deposit $2,000 into the plan.

In future years if you have a really good year you can contribute more than the $2,000, and in years in which you are a little hard up for excess dollars you can skip your deposit. But because insurance and commissions are involved, do not start the plan if you think you will only be contributing for one or two years.

The key to the plan is that similar to the standard IRA, all your money earns interest without any taxes coming out each year so your money grows faster than if it sat in a regular money market account.

Typical rates of interest are 8 to 9 percent.

The money you put into the plan is not a tax deduction. The deduction would be nice to have, but with the tax brackets below 30 percent that is not as big a factor as it once was.

And look what you get in exchange.

You keep the important feature that all your earnings are tax deferred.

You can make much higher annual contributions and save more than the $2,000.

You do not have to wait until you are 59 1/2 years to start withdrawing your money without a penalty like in a regular IRA.

When you do start to make withdrawals you will be able, at least under current tax law, to make them without having to declare the money on your tax return. In other words, the amounts you withdraw will appear as no-cost or low-cost loans against your reserves.

And before we give you an example, one final benefit to consider.

Remember, this Insured Retirement Account idea really has insurance backing it up. Therefore, if you were to die before you even started to make withdrawals or even after you started, a large death benefit will go to your survivors.

Okay, let us look at one example together.

Let us use a male, non-smoker, age 45. He is putting $2,000 into the plan from now to when he reaches 65. Based on the current return, at retirement he will be able to pull out about $7,850 per year and have a death benefit of a little more than $100,000 on top of that when he dies.

While the standard IRA could have grown just as much, dollars taken out of that plan are subject to taxes so more has to be taken out to end up with the same net tax-free amount. Therefore, after about 10 years of making withdrawals, the standard IRA will have been reduced to about one half of our new IRA plan. And remember the new plan still carries that $100,000 death benefit.

CHAPTER 10
SPECIAL INSURANCE NEEDS

NURSING HOME CARE — PROTECT YOURSELF NOW

While the debate goes on in the House and Senate over what benefits the elderly should receive through programs like Medicare, nothing is being done to solve the long-term nursing home crisis many elderly people face.

The current Medicare Catastrophic Act improves the coverage for what is called skilled care; that is, nursing home care which includes continuous medical supervision. This intensive care usually lasts only a short time anyway.

It is the custodial care, where the patient may need help with dressing, bathing or perhaps even eating, that accounts for about 90 percent of all nursing home stays.

And this kind of care can easily cost $100 a day. Multiply that times six months or even three years and you can quickly see how really "catastrophic" that can be.

Of course, most people don't really think it can happen to them. However, if I told you that one out of 70 cars would be involved in an auto accident in a given year, you would think that is quite high. Yet, it is estimated that two out of five people reaching the age of 65 will spend some time in a nursing home.

If it can be that expensive and the likelihood of it happening is very real, what is the best way to guard against financial ruin.

The answer is, of course, to buy a nursing home insurance policy.

Sounds simple enough and yet I see many elderly people like a lady (we'll call her Eileen) who came in to see me last week. Eileen is a widow with two children living up North. She has a nice portfolio, and we have been careful to skew it to produce a nice stream of income from conservative income securities.

But could her savings and portfolio income withstand a two-year stay in the type of nursing home she would feel comfortable in should she become impaired? The answer is no. She would soon have to start liquidating her principal.

Fortunately, she recognizes the potential problem, and for about $1,500 a year she now has peace of mind.

But a lot of time people will tell us, "Oh, I don't need to worry. My children will let me come and live with them."

Well, you may be right about their hearts being in the right place, but usually this is not a good solution because the children have their own lives, have no extra room, or have many other reasons for it not working.

Some people will admit they thought about the problem but never really looked into buying a specific insurance policy because they thought at their age it would be too expensive.

Well, certainly your age, health, and the amount of benefits and extras you want in your coverage will determine whether you pay something like $500 to $800 or $2,000 to $3,000 a year. But, I strongly urge people to at least consider some amount of coverage.

Who sells these policies and how do you make sure

you are getting the right one for you? It can be confusing. That's why I say, seek out someone who understands this area of your personal finances and will help you select the best coverage you can afford.

For example, some of the areas you need to examine closely are: Does the policy cover Alzheimer's disease? Do you have to go to a hospital before going to the nursing home? How much coverage a day should you buy? Is the policy guaranteed renewable? And the list goes on.

BIG STORMS CAN REQUIRE SPECIAL INSURANCE

Let's face it. Unless you are an insurance agent, the only time you want to discuss insurance is when it's too late.

One of the nation's worst storms in recent years, 1989's Hurricane Hugo, is a good example. Even as the storm approached, most people were not really sure if they had proper insurance to protect their homes from wind and water damage.

What you probably should do in the morning is make a call to your insurance agent who has your homeowners policy. He or she is in the best position to go over your present coverage and advise you what further protection you may want to buy.

Your insurance agent should start by explaining to you that damage from a major storm, like a hurricane, can be broken into two categories.

The most common is damage from a falling tree hitting your house — or your neighbor's house, patio furniture flying through your glass sliding doors or broken roof tiles. This kind of damage is all covered under your homeowners policy subject to your deductible.

Screen damage around a pool is very common and most policies will pay for the repair work. However, you should ask to be sure your policy does include this coverage. Keep your pool full of water because a pool that pops out of the ground due to water pressure buildup is not covered by insurance.

The second type of damage you might suffer, particularly if there is a lot of rain, is damage due to rising water. This kind of damage is usually only covered if you have a separate flood insurance policy.

Flood damage is broken into damage to the structure of a house or building and damage to contents inside. As a result, when you purchase flood insurance, you have to decide on the amount you want to cover in each area. The most you can purchase for the building is $185,000, and $60,000 is the most for your contents.

This limitation can be an important factor for those living in condominiums.

Too often, residents in a condominium ignore flood insurance coverage because the board of directors of their building has purchased coverage. But major damage could exceed the coverage purchased and individual condominium owners might find themselves assessed for the difference. If they have their own flood insurance policy, they can turn to it for the money.

The cost of flood insurance depends not only on the amount you purchase and the size of the deductible you ask for, but also, as you might expect, where you live.

To give you an example, for a median risk category, it would cost about $200 a year for $40,000 coverage on your house and $15,000 on contents inside.

There is no real incentive to shop this price because flood insurance is actually controlled through a federal program, and rates are set by the National Flood Insurance Program.

One thing you can do that could lower your cost is to have a survey done to see whether your house might sit a little higher within a category.

For example, people in the lowest levels (that is, highest risk categories) usually have to purchase flood insurance when they get their mortgage. However, if you have a survey taken, you might find while you are still classed in one of the highest rated categories, you can get a little cheaper rate.

To find out what flood zone or category you live in, contact your city, or if you do not reside in a city, the closest city to you will usually be able to help you.

And finally, if you are thinking of waiting until it looks certain that a major hurricane is about to hit the area before you buy a flood insurance policy, forget it. The National Flood Insurance Agency instructs all the insurance companies to stop selling the insurance five days before a storm is expected to hit.

SECTION TWO:
THE STOCK MARKET

CHAPTER 11
BROKERS

SHOPPING TIPS FOR FINDING THE RIGHT BROKER

Recently, I had the privilege of taking part in a panel discussion on how to help plan someone's finances. It all went very well, and I believe all three of us — the planners involved — gave sound advice. However, one woman asked a question that comes up so often, I thought I would try to address it with you.

This woman, saying she was rather new to the world of finance, asked how to go about selecting a broker or financial planner to handle her finances.

How about you? How did you get the person you have right now? Was it perhaps so long ago you cannot remember? If so, it could be a good sign of a good ongoing relationship with your advisor. Or did you just walk into the office and get the broker who was being assigned all walk-ins that day?

Perhaps your original broker left the firm and your account was arbitrarily assigned to someone else. That happens often. Whatever the situation, here is my answer to that woman's question of how do you find a financial planner.

First, there is no sure way to guarantee finding the perfect person. However, if you do a little homework both before and at the time of sitting down with the broker, you can improve your chances.

By all means, try, if you can, to find someone recommended by other people you have come to trust. This might be your attorney, accountant, life insurance agent, banker, neighbor or best friend. Ask whether the broker has moved around from firm to firm. Everyone has the right to change firms to improve his or her career, but someone who has been to three or four firms in a half dozen years should make you a little uneasy, to say the least.

Always, if you can, visit the office a couple of times as a casual observer. Try to be very inconspicuous. Sometimes this will give you an opportunity to see how brokers treat their clients when they think no one is around. Observe and listen to how they act just after they get off the telephone with another prospect or client.

If, by chance, the broker or financial advisor under consideration gives seminars or lectures, be sure to attend. If the person appears on a regular television show or radio program, tune in a number of times to try pick up their approach to things.

When you have finally made a selection and want to sit down with that person, you will get additional clues as to whether this person is for you or not.

For example, when you say you would like to sit down and talk about moving your account, does the advisor give you the time needed to make a decision or do you feel rushed? Granted, some planners/stockbrokers might be busier than others and therefore might prefer to see you very early or late in the day; but, if they do not give you enough time now, you probably will not get the attention after you have turned your account over to them either.

While you are talking, remember you are trying to find someone with whom you will be able to work with for years and years. You are looking for someone to match your personality. For example, you might be very aggressive and want someone who will follow your ideas and not question your thinking. Or it could be the reverse: you need someone who will be strong and tell you what should be done.

In general, however, most studies I have seen show the best relationships between client and advisor are those in which the two have similar values and tendencies.

It is also important that your future advisor is well educated and experienced in many different financial products. It is fine if the person specializes in certain areas. In fact, that may be the best. But you want to be sure your advisor does not think everything can be solved by buying municipal bonds, or common stock, or trading options, or real estate.

And, probably, as you leave your prospective broker's office, ask yourself whether the advisor seemed to be selling you something instead of explaining what you should do. In other words, was there give and take? Did he or she try to learn more about you? Does he or she seem to have empathy for your particular situation, or were you left with the impression he or she was trying to sell something, whether you needed it or not?

Understand, everyone I know is in this business to make money. However, there are different quality brokers and financial planners just as there are in any other field.

HOW TO GET RID OF BROKERS' ANNOYING CALLS

It is going on all across the country. The ring . . . ring of telephones, as literally thousands of stockbrokers try to smile and dial their way to prosperity.

Sometimes the calls carry the "importance" of coming from New York, or the person is calling on behalf of a "big" broker who gets on the line only after you express interest.

And, if it seems you are receiving a lot more unsolicited calls than before from stockbrokers to purchase stocks and bonds, or attend seminars, you are right.

Greed and fear in the investment business does not only apply to investors, but to Wall Streeters. Prior to October, 1987, calls were made, because for many, especially those newer in the business, it was relatively easy to cold-call his or her way into generating large volumes of commissions. But following the October market crash, business from the small investor has been off. Now the calls are being made as part of an attempt to try every possible means to reach out and grab someone's interest.

Brokerage firms are struggling to increase profitability. Those brokers that have stayed in the business after October's market crash are expected to reach certain levels of production by a certain length of time in the business. If they do not make the quota, they could be penalized by receiving a smaller percentage of the commissions they do generate. They could even find themselves asked to leave to make room for someone who is able to produce more business.

But not only new brokers or those struggling to stay in the business are the ones making all those telephone calls. Some of the most successful producers at any brokerage firm simply sit at their desk and call new people all day long with ideas.

In some cases, if it is a relatively new broker calling you, you might be better off dealing with them because with fewer clients you might have more of their attention. And a broker calling you late in the evening, at least tells you he or she is probably a pretty hard worker.

But what do you do when you get those calls at all hours of the day and evening, and you really are not interested, but the broker calling does not seem to want to let you go? It seems as if some of them have been taught not to take no for an answer.

How do you get off the line with these people if you have no interest? I have talked to a number of brokers, as well as people who have received such calls. Here is what seems to work and not work.

One thing you cannot do is say you do not have any money to invest, because, chances are the salesperson knows the street or area he or she is calling and has figured out you have money somewhere, or you would not be living where you do.

It also won't work to tell the caller you already have a broker, because he or she will simply tell you that you should have two brokers.

And do not say all your money is tied up in certificates of deposit, because, they will ask you when will that money become available and call you back on that date.

You can try saying you only do business with people you meet face to face and would want to visit the broker at his or her office first. Now you control the situation.

If you are being really hounded by a broker who won't take no for an answer, you can be very agreeable with everything the broker says on the telephone and then say you would like to read up on it a little and to send something in the mail. When they call back and ask whether you like what you read, you simply repeat your request to see something in the mail proclaiming you did not receive the earlier material.

The problems with these methods, however, is you are wasting a lot of your time listening to the whole pitch and wasting a lot of the broker's time, who is, after all, trying to earn a living.

The best answer I heard, was from a woman who says she tells callers her son or daughter is a stockbroker. This works even better than saying you yourself are a broker, because it avoids getting into a possible discussion with "someone else in the business".

CHAPTER 12
MEASURING THE ECONOMY

YOUR KEYS TO MEASURING THE ECONOMY

There is a line from a popular cowboy song that says, "Mamas, don't let your babies grow up to be cowboys," the inference being it is a hard and miserable way to make a living.

Today, a lot of economists are probably thinking that job could not be a whole lot harder than trying to predict where the U.S. economy is going.

Unlike weather forecasters who casually tell you on Monday that the sunny weekend they promised ended in rain because the wind currents shifted, and then move right along with a new forecast, economists stay employed only as long as they can tell the captains of the various mega ships out there what course to chart.

If economists are wrong and the corporate ship gets damaged by putting out bonds at 12 percent instead of waiting to put them out at nine percent, or the company spends $5 million on a capital expansion, only to find that the economy is going down the tubes, they are out of a job.

But just how difficult can an economist's job be, you might ask, knowing how our government surveys and charts every little economic thing?

Look at these summaries of economic headlines taken from the Wall Street Journal not long ago over a three-day span.

* Leading Indicators slid .6 percent in January, but December's figure was revised to up .3 percent, rather than down .2 percent.
* Construction outlays fell 2.9 percent in January.
* Factory orders fell .6 percent in January.
* Home sales fell 9 percent in January to a five-year low.
* Oil prices slipped to a 10-week low.
* Car sales surged 24 percent in late February.
* Major retailers posted weak sales for February.

Question:

Is the economy moving up, and perhaps so fast we shall see higher interest rates, or is it sliding, and perhaps so quickly we will shortly see signs of a recession, or at least lower interest rates to help stimulate the economy?

Of the above seven reports, six point to a slowing of the economy and only one, the big increase in auto sales, supports a robust economy. But if it was as simple as adding up two columns and seeing which one had the most, economists would not be paid NFL-type salaries.

Take the first item, the one about the leading indicators being down about a half percent in January. That may be, but notice how the government has revised the figure for December, from a drop in the index to a gain.

That is particularly important because many economists believe three down months of leading indicators in a row will almost certainly bring on a recession of some sort. In this example, December would have been the third month. Now the string has been broken.

Here is another example of why these reports should sometimes be taken with a grain of salt. Look at the construction figures. The reports say construction spending and home sales were both down in January. However, common sense would tell you if interest rates stay where they are or even drop a little, housing activity is going to pick up as people take advantage of relatively low mortgages.

That big increase in auto sales? That one certainly needs to be watched in the next month or two. If you get car sales and home-buying activity running too fast, it does not take long for salaries to starting jumping up. And all the reports, indictors and data are not nearly as crucial a signal that the economy is running too fast as when contract negotiations are settled quickly and for far higher wages than were expected.

Remember, like a ball bouncing down the stairs, the direction is down, even though, along the way the ball bounces up. So while most economists and brokerage firms go on predicting that the long-term trend in interest rates is downward, let us keep an eye out for danger signals.

HOW TO PREDICT INTEREST RATE DIRECTIONS

Whether or not you are an investor in the stock market, it pays these days to know which way interest rates are heading.

Over the last several years, we have vividly experienced how rising interest rates can ultimately choke off a bustling economy. As money gets more expensive to borrow, both corporations and you, the consumer, tend to spend less. That means fewer goods are needed. Then we have layoffs, and, of course, these layoffs further dampen the economy, and the cycle feeds on itself.

But whether you are thinking of buying a home, or you are an investor waiting for corporate profits to improve, like it or not, the direction of interest rates is important to you.

For this reason, economists are constantly being asked to project which way they see interest rates moving. Today, as is typically the case, some experts believe interest rates will move up several hundred basis points, and others think rates have further to fall.

(In bond and interest rate jargon, one hundred basis points equal one percent. For example, a movement of 150 basis points would mean interest rates have gone from 10 to 11 1/2 percent.)

Economists are a lot like engineers. They draw their conclusions after studying reams of data. Unfortunately, the information they work with is often months old, and even the current data often does not always accurately reflect what is really going on.

That is why you constantly hear on the news that some figures announced last month are being revised, or that economists are ignoring certain figures released today, because they think the figures are an aberration.

Personally, I am slow to follow only one guru when it comes to interest rates. Even if an economist has been correct three times in a row, or even fives times, it does not mean he or she will always be right. At some point, what actually happens will be the opposite of what they predict. Whether you are investing your last $20,000 or just another $100,000, do not bet on just what one well-known person is saying, no matter what his or her track record has been.

If you want to know more about interest rates, you might start paying attention to the data that comes out regularly from various government offices. You can start to monitor a lot of the same data economists see.

Here is a list of some of the more meaningful government reports.

The Consumer Price Index, one of the most widely recognized reports, comes out about the third week of each month. The index represents the average change in prices of a lot of everyday things we use such as food, clothing, shelter, fuel, transportation and medical care. If that index moves up very much, the market tends to go down, because investors see it as indication of inflation.

When the economy seems to be running too fast, steps are taken to slow it down. Historically, one of those steps has been to tighten the money supply. If the supply of money is tightened, banks have less to lend; they charge more for what money they have available, and thus, interest rates climb. Rates will eventually rise to the point where most people will not find it attractive to borrow money. At that point, the expansion period of the economy comes to an end.

Other indicators that the economy is moving too fast and needs to be slowed down include: rising agricultural prices, a big increase in the number of single-family housing starts and a big increase in retail sales.

Conversely, if these indicators move down, the Federal Reserve Board may make money available to corporations and consumers at lower interest rates to encourage us to spend more.

Watch early each month for employment figures to see whether employment is increasing or decreasing. If unemployment seems to be up, then you can expect the bond markets to go up, because investors will see it as a sign that the Federal Reserve Board cannot raise interest rates.

Each quarter, the Gross National Product announcement is made. Because this is one of the most encompassing measures of economic activity, it almost always causes the stock market to react.

There are actually dozens of reports announced each month. If you start watching some of these figures routinely, you will begin to develop favorites. For example, I like to watch the newspapers for labor union wage settlements. Other people like watching the balance of payments.

A closing thought: Be careful not to judge the country's economy simply by what is going on in your household or your geographic area. I remember an economics professor telling us that we tend to react like the fellow who hears about his neighbor being laid off, so he says there is a recession going on. But if the fellow himself gets laid off, then, by gosh, the country must be in a depression.

CHAPTER 13
DIVERSIFICATION AND RISK

ASSET ALLOCATION ALWAYS MAKES SENSE

Proper allocation of assets has long been a basic tenent in planning one's finances. However, since the dramatic upheaval in the stock market in 1987, the concept seems to be attracting even more attention.

Putting various percentages of a person's financial holdings into a variety of investments maximizes return, while protecting against unusual market volatility.

Or, to put it more simply, it is not wise to put all your eggs in one basket.

In any event, "asset allocation" is the latest buzzword among those in financial services.

Indeed, positioning your assets into different areas, where each product's weakness can be compensated by another investment, is sound planning.

For example, say you want a lot of income-producing real estate, because you like the quarterly checks and the inflation hedge real estate has historically provided. However, you realize that real estate's major weakness is its illiquidity. Therefore, a percentage of your overall portfolio should be kept in short-term paper or money market funds.

Take another example we see all the time.

A client, let's say her name is Lillian, sells her insurance business and retires. Lillian figures that, if she puts all the money from the sale of her business into long-term corporate or municipal bonds, she will have enough income to live comfortably the rest of her life.

Bonds are liquid, and they do give a nice return. However, they offer no growth. Thus, any amount of inflation will steadily decrease their worth.

To balance this portfolio, Lillian needs to have a certain percentage of her money invested in something like common stock or real estate to protect her buying power down the road.

This way, if, after a number of years, Lillian's bond portfolio has lost value because interest rates went higher, her real estate investment should have performed very well and be worth a nice profit.

She could then sell the bonds and take a loss, sell the real estate for a gain, and thus keep the value of her portfolio where it was.

Someone else might have wanted to balance this portfolio with gold. After all, gold does seem to appreciate when inflation rises.

But there is one problem with gold. It does not produce any income. As an inflation hedge, gold is probably best used as a small percentage of a person's total portfolio.

In reality, the amount you put into bonds, common stock, aggressive growth funds, precious metals, limited partnerships, or some other type of investment mode depends on what your main objective is.

For example, do you want rapid growth, regardless of the risk? Or are you interested mainly in income, as opposed to overall growth?

The really good portfolio planners are a little like top chefs. They do not use rigid percentages, forcing people to conform. They look at each situation and, after considering a person's age, health, attitude toward risk, income needs and amount to invest, mix up an appropriate recipe.

DIVERSIFICATION SAFEGUARDS AGAINST UNKNOWN

If you were invited up north during the late summer or early fall to spend a few days with a friend, you would probably pack some rather summery things and a couple of heavy sweaters and coat.

And after you got there, chances are the weather would be either gorgeous and you would be upset with yourself for not packing more light things instead of being stuck with those heavy sweaters and coat; or the weather would be freezing, and you would wish you had had enough common sense to have packed all the heavy things you owned and left the light things behind.

But, let's face it. When you left you could not be sure what the weather would be like so you had to diversify your wardrobe. You could not take the chance of guessing and being wrong.

And so it is, in a way, when you diversify your financial portfolio.

We all agree it makes sense to diversify when you cannot be guaranteed what will happen down the road. But investors tend to get upset when some of their investments put in the portfolio for diversification do not keep up with the current trends.

For example, when real estate was going gangbusters in 1979 and other assets, such as stocks, were performing somewhat lackadaisically, everyone wanted to have all their capital in real estate.

A few years later, people wanted their dollars in the stock market where the pickings looked easy.

If you are aggressive and can take the risk, you certainly do want to be moving from market to market to be where the action is. But moving the wrong way at the wrong time will cause you severe financial hardship. Diversifying protects you from winding up at the wrong end as the investment pendulum swings.

Sometimes the swings amount to short-term market timing. Other times the swings are major trends that take years to evolve.

A classic example of the latter was during a period a few years ago when the message was that energy cost in this country would be basically moving higher over the next decade. With that in mind, it was prudent to position some of your dollars in oil and gas assets. Many investors purchased common stock in oil companies, bought limited partnerships owning or drilling for more oil, and some purchased contracts on oil futures.

No one conceived oil prices would fall as far as they did and stay down so long.

Certainly not giant U.S. Steel, as it was still known back in 1982, when it paid a fortune to buy Marathon Oil. Neither did Chevron Oil, which had to fight a fierce battle and pay such a high price for Gulf Oil in 1984.

What the price of oil will be six months or six years from now is uncertain. But if you invest in a quality company with good reserves and good management, then even while those dollars in your portfolio are underperforming some of your other investments, they are a hedge against suddenly rising prices and perhaps a falling economy.

I still remember the headline, "Real Estate: Why the Bad Gets Worse", appearing in respected *Business Week* in late 1975. A couple of years later, real estate was the place to be.

How you diversify your portfolio — whether you use hard assets such as gold and silver, inflation-sensitive assets such as real estate, or whatever else — depends, of course, on your own individual situation. But remember, all your assets are not expected to perform at the same rate.

DEFINE YOUR DEFINITION OF RISK

"Risk", as a word, has many elements when it comes to investing.

There is the obvious, "How safe is my investment?" But there are also several other less obvious, but certainly equally important, aspects.

It is only human nature, but I suspect that if you took a room full of people, and asked each of them to explain or define how they saw risk, each would have a different answer.

Risk is a crucial factor in investing, and we need to understand it.

Sometimes, those we think should not be too concerned with risk turn out to be the most safety conscious of all.

For example, I remember some months ago giving a guest lecture on financial planning to a group of doctors. Now you would probably think, here is a group who will be more interested in maximizing their dollars and taking bigger risks.

Yet, when the meeting was over and everyone handed in his or her sheet of paper indicating what areas they would like to have additional information on, the most checked box was for information on the use of zero-coupon treasury certificates, an investment that many consider to be among the most conservative of all investments.

Another aspect of risk that needs to be addressed is your personal view of risk.

Some people are drawn to risk. They need it in everything they do. They are great risk takers. Show them the slower, steadier way of getting somewhere, and they will say "thank you," and proceed to take their chances with a faster route.

This person can buy an index option and even if it goes down by the end of the trading day, he or she will have no trouble sleeping. Another person might finally be convinced that a utility stock has a safe dividend and that the stock will go up gradually. But should it slip down a half a point from where he or she purchased it, they are immediately on the telephone to their broker wondering how they could have been talked into such a risky investment.

The amount of money or capital you have behind you will affect how you see things. Take the above example. If the person buying those shares of stock needed those same dollars to pay next month's rent or mortgage, then all at once we agree even a utility or an oil stock was too risky of an investment.

If you look at just about everyone's portfolio, you will normally see a range of investments spreading from low risk to moderate risk to high risk. What is interesting is that the scale starts and stops at different places for different people.

Someone's idea of moderate risk might be someone else's low end of the scale.

So, whenever you sit down with your investment adviser, especially for the first time, make sure you define what kind of investments you see as risky and which you consider very conservative.

SENSIBLE DIVERSIFICATION IDEAS

Some lessons are so hard to learn.

A fundamental principal of asset or portfolio building is diversification. Yet, our human nature drives us to go where the action is at the moment.

How many times have you heard, "Don't put all your eggs in one basket"? We know that is true. But how long can you be expected to adhere to your game plan when everything you see and read says to be invested in XYZ?

Real estate seemed to be the guaranteed way to unlimited riches at the turn of the decade.

Then, after interest rates had fallen for about a year, investors started pouring dollars into income-producing mutual funds.

Three years into the interest rate slide, the amount of money going into income funds was more than triple that being invested in common stock funds.

Then in April of 1987, interest rates suddenly shot upward and investors in fixed-yield securities lost out. But there were a lot of theories about how it would not happen again, so it was not until interest rates jumped up again in late summer, that investors decided they would rather be in the stock market which was continuing to hit new highs. Income funds were out of favor and stocks were the place to be invested.

Then came the savage and unprecedented attack on the stock market. It was like watching a lone swimmer under attack from a huge shark. People scrambled out of the market. The terror on their faces told you they would not be going back in for some time.

And what was suddenly looking attractive again? You guessed it. Corporate, municipal and government securities. The bonds gained back a nice piece of what they lost, as interest rates suddenly dropped lower.

If you accept the axiom that you cannot always be in the right spot at the right time, you must practice diversification. Switch percentages around, but stay spread out.

Within these percentages in your portfolio, you can even do more things to protect your principal.

Say you have a portfolio of common stocks worth about $100,000. You do not think the decline in the market will go much further, but you are wondering whether you might just be wrong. One thing you can do is purchase put options.

Buying put options on the market is by itself very risky. It is a high-leverage investment in which you control a lot of stock with just a few dollars. However, in this case you would be spending a small amount of money relative to the total amount of your portfolio.

Let us look at an example. I am going to round the figures off to make it easier to follow. If you like the idea, you will want to make sure you fully understand options, including their risk. Before investing you should ask for and read the Options Risk and Disclosure booklet. You also will need to have exact prices to see how it will work with your portfolio.

But for the purposes of discussion, let us say the OEX market index is at 225 and to purchase one put option from now until the third Friday in December costs $1,200. This means it will cost you $1,200 to control about $22,500 of stocks. Divide this amount into your portfolio and round up. ($100,000/22,500 = 4.4. Round up equals 5.) Therefore, you would buy five put options.

This means for a cost of $6,000, you now have a position that will benefit you if the market goes down.

Say the market continues to fall. Your portfolio of common stocks is going to lose value. However, your puts are going to increase in value. The loss in your stocks will be offset by the gain in the put options. Of course, if the market goes up, your investment in the puts will become worthless, but your portfolio will more than have made up for the loss.

If you are not holding common stocks but instead have a lot of dollars invested in the government funds and you are afraid of rising interest rates, consider this diversification strategy.

Transfer a small percentage of the money you have in the government funds into zero-coupon treasuries. While these dollars will not be paying you any current income, they will be compounding within themselves, and when they mature you will have made back the principal being lost elsewhere.

Say you decided you could give up about 10 percent of your invested $100,000 dollars in a government fund. You purchase $10,000 worth of zero-coupon treasuries that will come due 15 years from now and be worth $40,000 no matter what. It should help you enjoy your current income from the rest of your money knowing you have this assets builder working for you on the side.

CHAPTER 14
USE OF MARGIN

TAKING ADVANTAGE OF TAX DEDUCTIBLE MARGIN INTEREST

Traditionally, people think of using margin in a brokerage account as a way to purchase additional shares of a security without putting up more cash. And while this is still the most common use, many investors are learning another benefit.

They have discovered, with a little planning, they are able to use a margin account to give them a quick loan that has greater tax deductibility than a regular consumer loan, and the resulting savings can be significant.

Brokerage firms are usually happy to allow you to borrow an amount equal to half the value of your common stocks and 85 to 90 percent of the value of your government bonds. These loans are easy to make, have no origination fees and can be paid back whenever you would like.

Do not forget though, that you have borrowed against your securities and therefore, if their market value should fall considerably, you could be asked to pay back some of the principal or otherwise add to the value of your account.

The Tax Reform Act of 1986 attacked interest on consumer loans for automobiles, credit card purchases, etc. The law said only 40 percent of such interest expense will be deductible in 1988, and the percentage will continue to decline until it reaches zero in 1991.

But while the tax changes also affected the deductibility of interest paid for borrowed funds from a brokerage account, the change left intact one major difference.

Under the prior law, you were allowed to borrow money against your security holdings and deduct all of that interest, up to an amount equal to the amount of income you made from your securities, plus another $10,000.

With the change in the tax law, the amount of interest you pay that exceeds the amount of income your account is bringing in, is now only partially deductible (20% in 1989 and 10% in 1990). Starting in 1991, none of the amount over what matches your investment income will be deductible.

However, you are able to deduct all of the interest that is covered, or equals, the income earned from your account.

In other words, you have an account made up of a few utility stocks, a corporate bond, a small government mutual fund and a money market position. Total income for the year including the interest and dividends is $4,000. That means you can borrow against your account and deduct any interest expense up to $4,000, plus that percent of $10,000 we talked about.

But you must be careful in how you use the interest. It must be for investment purposes and not some other consumer purchase.

Let us take a look at an example.

An uncle has passed away leaving you $50,000. You and your spouse have talked it over, and you have decided you will purchase a new car that will run you $25,000. But you also realize you need to invest some of that money in a diversified portfolio of high quality stocks and bonds. It might be retirement you are worried about or your child's education.

If you buy $45,000 of securities and take $5,000 for the down payment on the car, you will be paying interest on $20,000. If the interest was 10 percent, to make it nice and easy, that would be $2,000 of interest of which only 20 percent, or $400, will be recognized as a deduction in 1989. (This will drop further in 1990).

If, on the other hand, you pay cash for the car and set up your $45,000 portfolio with the remaining $25,000, you would increase your taxable deductions and get what amounts to a rebate.

Let us say the interest on the margin account is also going to cost you 10 percent. In reality, it would probably be less than the rate you would pay for the consumer debt, but let us use the same rate to make our example simpler. So you again have an interest expense of $2,000.

But our $45,000 portfolio might well be producing dividends and interest of at least $2,000. Now, under the current tax law, we can deduct all of the interest expense up to what our investment income equals and then a percent after that. That means all of the $2,000 interest expense would be a deductible item on your 1040 return.

In both examples, you have a car and a $45,000 portfolio, and you have borrowed $20,000. But in one case, all of the interest is deductible, while in the other only a small portion is deductible.

The key here is that had you first paid cash for the securities and then borrowed the money for a consumer expense, the government would have disallowed most of the deduction, because it would have been viewed as a consumer expenditure loan.

DON'T LET MARGIN GET OUT OF CONTROL

A potentially dangerous situation has been developing. But as with many other changes we have undergone in the past decade, the opportunities allow for good to come of it or a great deal of bad.

Two of the major forces in investing have taken steps separately, that when combined, could have a major impact on your future.

Over the past couple of years, many Wall Street firms have been telling their brokers they are expensive to keep, given all their demands of office space, secretarial assistance and research. Marginal brokers have been served notice, they must either produce more or expect to keep less of the commissions they earn.

Many brokers trying to reach certain levels of sales production each month are going to find themselves needing just a couple of more trades to get into the next level. That is incentive. Controlled, that is what selling is all about. Uncontrolled, and you have all the wrongs of this industry staring you right in the face.

Now, to add to the potential danger, the Securities and Exchange Commission has recently ruled that fully paid mutual fund shares will now be marginable like regular common stock.

And remember, we already have more and more financial institutions telling you your home, which for so many is their one true redeeming asset, is in effect marginable.

The ability to margin or borrow against certain assets is not in itself wrong. In fact, properly used, it can be a great assist in building wealth.

The danger lies in the fact that many financially inexperienced homeowners or owners of mutual funds are going to be told if they borrow against these paid-up assets and place the money into such and such, they will make a lot more money.

The fact is, yes, it is possible, but there is also the potential for catastrophe. What happens to your assets and living style if you are sold a losing investment that you borrowed money to pay for?

I remember back in the mid-70s when some brokers were getting people to buy large amounts of treasury bonds on margin on the promise of a sure, no-lose scheme.

If I remember, it went something like this.

You bought a large block of treasury bonds with just a tiny amount of cash. You margined the rest; that is, borrowed from the brokerage firm for the rest. At the time, margin cost on the borrowed money was about 10 percent. However, the government bond you purchased was paying about 11 1/2 percent.

You were told, without any risk, you had a spread of 1 1/2 percent on whatever amount of treasuries you purchased. And you were told you could close out your position at any time.

What the salesperson did not bother to explain is that everything was hunky-dory as long as interest rates did not go up. Because once they did, here is what would happen.

The margin interest rate you are paying starts moving up to a point where the spread between it and the treasury bond is no longer profitable. In fact, the cost of the borrowed money can go way beyond what the treasury bond is paying you. So you tell the broker you do not like what is happening and would like to close out your portfolio.

Well, er, ah, yes, you can close out your position, but the treasury bond is not worth as much since interest rates have gone up. And, in fact, the brokerage firm is calling you for additional money to make up for the loss in value of the treasury bonds.

At this point, our imaginary investor has no more money available to meet the margin call. He never thought he would need to. Remember, this was a safe transaction using government guaranteed treasuries.

As interest rates rise, the squeeze gets unbearable. The person stands to lose a lot.

In the case of homes, there is the so-called reverse mortgage. This is where a couple, in cooperation with a financial institution, makes a deal allowing them to pull out dollars from the equity in their house on a monthly basis with the agreement that when they die, instead of the house going to the relative, it will go to the financial institution.

There is some merit to this plan. There are many cases where elderly people, having little or no assets outside of their home and hardly able to get by on a day-to-day basis, can find this useful.

But there are also those plans that allow you to establish a credit line on the asset value of your house that then allows you to put those dollars in places that can bite your hand. This could spell trouble to a lot of innocent, somewhat unknowledgeable people.

The same goes for allowing mutual funds to be margined. We have created the potential for many unsuspecting people to be talked into margining their few relatively safe assets on a bet that they will do better.

The situation seems fraught with danger, and I believe it will become all the more important that you are sure of who is doing your investing and that they are telling you both sides of the story.

HOW MARGIN WILL MAGNIFY YOUR RESULTS

A lot of investors are making use of margin accounts, whereby they invest in the market using borrowed money.

Buying securities with margin gives investors the opportunity to dramatically increase the rate of return on their investment. But because of the increased leverage, buying with margin can also be devastating.

Over the years I have found many investors do not understand margin. There are those that use it, not fully aware of extra risk they have taken on. There are others who turn a deaf ear at the mere sound of the word, perhaps missing out on good opportunities to increase their rate of return.

Let us take a look at perhaps the most common use of margin.

For whatever reason, you believe stock XYZ is well positioned to move up in the next number of weeks or months. The stock is trading at $20 per share, and you buy 500 shares for a total outlay of $10,000, forgetting about commission cost.

Let us say you were right and XYZ moves up to $28 within a couple of months. You sell and have a $4,000 profit on your $10,000 again forgetting commissions. That would be a nice profit of 40 percent in a short time.

However, if you had instead bought twice as many shares of XYZ using a margin account at a brokerage firm, you would have owned 1,000 shares and earned $8,000. While you still have to figure the cost of the extra shares, plus the interest charged by the brokerage firm for borrowing half of the amount, you have nevertheless made roughly an $8,000 profit on your $10,000 investment, giving you about an 80% rate of return in the same length of time.

Remember the popular Clint Eastwood movie, *The Good, The Bad And The Ugly*? Well, that was the "good" of using a margin account. Here is the "bad and ugly".

You buy the extra shares, paying interest to the brokerage firm on a daily basis for the amount of money the firm is lending you. Usually the more you borrow — such as $100,000 versus $10,000, — the lower your rate of interest.

Let us say your stock is not really doing anything. It is just sitting there.

Pretty soon the money you have spent in interest amounts to more than what the stock is ever going to increase by. In cases like that, you probably should review why you purchased the stock and decide whether it is worth holding on to it.

The ugly you will discover is when the stock takes a nose dive. Now you have a loss on twice as many shares, and you are still paying the daily interest.

You might be tempted to stick it out, thinking the market, or at least your stock, is about to rebound. But there is a stock exchange requirement that says that while you can originally start off your account by paying for just half the stock you buy, you can never let the value of the stock position fall to less than 30 percent of the total original value of the purchase.

If you do, you will be notified that you must either deposit additional cash or securities to bring your value back up. Failure to do so usually results in a sell-out of your position. And if the stock rebounds the next day, you are simply out of luck.

There is no denying from a brokerage's point of view, margining trades can be profitable. The firm very often ends up selling twice the number of securities it would otherwise. That makes for larger commissions. And the money the brokerage firm lends also generates income.

To control the use of margin somewhat, the exchange requires that trades worth less than $2,000 be fully paid for. Also, many low priced stocks are not marginable. The exchange does allow some mutual funds to be used as marginable securities. That is, you can borrow against the value of these funds. But the fact that you do this, of course, does not mean that you should.

Margin in itself does not make a trade good or bad. It only magnifies what is there.

CHAPTER 15
OPTIONS

STOCK INSURANCE FIGHTS INDIGESTION

Here we go again. Just when we started to get our confidence back about the stock market, along comes some negative news, and the Dow Jones Industrials are in a nose dive again.

Will it stop in a day or two, as some economists are saying, or is this just the beginning of a long descent?

If you have even a tiny bit of doubt in your mind about the future health of your stock, you might want to look into buying some insurance on your portfolio.

No, the Met and New York Life do not sell this kind of insurance. You have to see your stockbroker for it.

Probably the simplest type of investment insurance you can buy is an "index put". This will act as a hedge against your stock investments, should the market fall further over the next several weeks or months.

Puts are stock options in which you bet that the price of a stock will go down. A put gives you the right to put — that is, sell — someone a stock at a specified price within a predetermined length of time — no matter what the price actually is in the market.

Say your portfolio has a dozen or more stocks. Rather than purchase a put option on each and every stock, it is a lot easier to purchase one of the index puts that represent a number of stocks.

For example, if your portfolio is made up primarily of blue chip securities, you might use the Major Market Index, called the XMI, which is composed of 20 stocks, almost all of which are in the Dow Jones Industrial Average. If you wanted something a little broader, you could use the S&P 100 Index, called the OEX, which is composed of large capitalized stocks.

Let's look at an example involving the OEX.

At any given time, the OEX option will have a dozen or so strike prices, that is, the dollar price at which you could purchase or sell. Say the index is trading at 270 with the Dow Jones Industrials at 2250. A number of option strike prices will be listed at below the 270, and a number will be offered above 270 Never mind why the index is at 270; just understand that the value of the option, which represents where the market is now, will either go up or down, depending on what the stock market does.

If you think the market is going down, you would buy one or more puts on the 270 option. You could also work with one of the other higher or lower options.

The closer the put option strike price is to where the index currently is valued, the more protection you are buying, and — as with all insurance — the more it will cost you.

To really do a good job of balancing the worth of your portfolio with index put options, you probably need to buy several. As a handy guide to figuring out how many you need to purchase, take the value of your portfolio — say $200,000 — and divide it by the put option, times 100. We chose the 270 option, so we would divide 200,000 by 27,000 and come up with 7 1/2. So you ought to purchase at least seven options to insure your portfolio.

Like all insurance, this costs you money. You might

purchase seven options at $450, for $3,150, excluding commissions. If the market ends up rising, your put options will expire worthless.

That is the bad news. The good news is, if the market does indeed go up, your portfolio will reach a new high.

Naturally, before you do any trading in options, you should fully understand the risks involved. And you should consult with someone knowledgeable to determine which option you should use and how much you should pay for it.

CHAPTER 16
MUTUAL FUNDS

WHEN YOUR MUTUAL FUND CAN BE TAXING

Mutual funds have been very popular because of their relatively good performance and the promotion they get by thousands of stockbrokers.

And if you own shares of a mutual fund, there will come a day when you will want to cash in on some of your profits or perhaps switch to another fund. And when you do, if you have not kept accurate records, you or your accountant may have trouble figuring out your taxes. Especially if you have been reinvesting your interest and capital gains distributions.

There is a tendency for many mutual fund investors to sink some money into the one or two of their choice and then walk away from the details, instructing the fund manager to reinvest all earnings.

Very often these investors do not keep accurate records of additional new monies committed to the fund. Seldom does this investor keep all the statements showing what distributions have been made and at what price new shares were purchased.

The IRS allows you to figure what your gain or loss is by using one of two methods. If you have kept accurate records, when you sell some of your shares, you can match them up with specific shares you purchased earlier. This will allow you to take big gains or losses in taxable years, when it will suit your overall tax picture better.

If you have not kept accurate records, the IRS will allow you to use the averaging method.

Like the name implies, you merely add up all the money that you have invested, along with all your reinvested earnings, and divide by the total number of shares you now have. This will be your cost basis. The difference between that and the price you get for the shares when they are sold, will be your gain or loss. If you held the shares for more than six months, it is a long-term transaction.

For example, you invest $10,000 in a good growth and income fund. During the next number of years, you received $5,000 in capital gains that you reinvested plus $3,000 of interest that you also reinvested. Now you want to sell all your fund shares.

You would subtract from your total proceeds the $10,000 plus $5,000 plus $3,000.

A couple of other points to remember:

Even if you have all your earnings from interest and capital gains distributions reinvested, you will still be taxed on the earnings. The government says you earned it, and even though you elected not to take it out to spend, you did receive it, and you will be taxed. A lot of people falsely believe if they do not take the money out, it works as a deferred taxation plan does.

Something else to keep in mind:

While virtually every mutual fund is in some kind of family of funds that allows you to switch shares around within the fund without paying a new commission each time, you will trigger a taxable event when you move from one fund to the other, no matter how close the family members are to each other.

Some enterprising individuals have used this to tell investors it is a way to reduce the up-front sales commission they might have to pay.

Here is how it works.

Say you want to go into XYZ's government fund for income. But it has a front-end charge of 5 percent. You buy shares in XYZ's growth fund and pay the 5-percent charge. Then a couple of days later, you sell your shares of the growth fund and move into the government fund where you wanted to be all the time.

If you bought the shares at $10 with the 5-percent charge, the shares would be bidding $9.50 right away. Now, you switch at that price, triggering a short-term loss of 50 cents per share. You are now into the fund you wanted to be, and although you have paid 50 cents commission, you have also created a short-term taxable loss of 50 cents that will save you on your tax bill.

Of course, if everyone started doing this, it would drive the system wacky. Some funds protect themselves by limiting how soon you can move in and out.

WHY HOPPERS FINISH LAST

If you have been in the stock market any length of time, you would have heard the old joke that the way to make money is to buy low and sell high.

No one can argue with that.

The trick, of course, is knowing when it is low and when it is high. All the technical rules and all the common sense arguments in the world could not explain why last October one day the Dow Jones figure represented a low and more buying should be done, and a few days later that figure was suddenly seen as astronomically high and stocks should have been sold.

It is no wonder then, many investors a long time ago accepted the fact there are factors involved that cannot be measured or calculated with any accuracy and therefore simply invest in a good quality balanced mutual fund and stay put.

Well, recently one of these funds showed what would have happened had you put $10,000 in their fund January 1, 1975, and let it re-invest right through to December 31, 1987. It would have accumulated $132,847. That is a 1,229 percent return over the 13 years. This is not an uncommon long-term return for a well-managed balanced mutual fund.

Granted, this figure was calculated disregarding taxes, sales commissions and having all the return invested each year. But even if you reduce the total return to compensate for all those unique advantages, it would still work out to be a nice return.

But what we really wanted you to see was how this simple approach would compare to someone who each year moved their investment to the top performing mutual fund the year before.

You know how so many of the financial publications today publish ratings and rankings of the top performing fund each quarter and for the year? Well, it would be someone that took $10,000 and said, Fund XYZ was the top performer in 1974, rising 10.9 percent. Therefore, I am going to put my $10,000 in fund XYZ January 1, 1975. Then next January they took what their money was now worth and invested it with the winner for 1975, and so forth. Again, no allowance was made for taxes or sales commissions.

Well, at the end of 13 years, their $10,000 had grown to just $52,680, or 427 percent according to the study.

And when you look at the breakdown year by

year, you can see why the hopper did not make as much headway. So often the winner became a loser the following year.

In the year:	#1 Fund's Return:	The Next Year:	Its Total Return:	Your $10,000 (NO FEES) was worth:
1974	10.9%	1975	−24.1%	$ 7,590 on 12/31/75
1975	184.1%	1976	46.5%	$11,119 on 12/31/76
1976	72.5%	1977	19.9%	$13,332 on 12/31/77
1977	51.5%	1978	27.6%	$17,012 on 12/31/78
1978	58.9%	1979	−23.4%	$13,031 on 12/31/79
1979	187.3%	1980	78.9%	$23,312 on 12/31/80
1980	93.9%	1981	−13.2%	$20,235 on 12/31/81
1981	48.2%	1982	81.3%	$36,686 on 12/31/82
1982	81.3%	1983	24.8%	$45,785 on 12/31/83
1983	58.1%	1984	−28.0%	$32,965 on 12/31/84
1984	48.6%	1985	26.5%	$41,701 on 12/31/85
1985	69.6%	1986	11.4%	$46,455 on 12/31/86
1986	77.8%	1987	13.4%	$52,680 on 12/31/87

426.8% Net Return

Mutual funds are sold by prospectus only. Read carefully before you invest or send money.

CHAPTER 17
BONDS

A SIMPLE FORMULA TO CALCULATE BOND YIELD

There is a handy formula you can use to calculate bond yield to maturity.

I have already pointed out how the exact yield to maturity of any bond, whether it is selling at a discount or a premium, is calculated by computers and tables to reflect the value of all the individual coupon payment periods, with a discount factor.

But, while the exact figure on a bond may be necessary before taking action on it, a simple formula can help for those times you are reviewing your current bond portfolio, and you have a number of bonds selling at a discount and you are considering trading them for a different investment.

Before we present the formula for calculating yield to maturity, let me say, it looks more difficult than it is. So let's take it through, step by step, and you will have a handy guide for future reference.

Here is how to find the yield to maturity of a bond trading at a premium.

Yield to maturity equals A divided by B. A is the annual coupon interest, less the value of the total premium, divided by the number of years to maturity. B is the current price of the bond, plus its value at maturity, divided by 2.

Now, let's run through an example together. If you can find a pencil and put down the formula as we go through it, you will find it rather easy.

For example, we want to know the yield to maturity of a bond with an 8 percent coupon, 10 years left to maturity and currently priced at $1,040.

Remember, yield to maturity equals value A divided by value B.

A is going to be $80 (annual interest bond pays) less the result of dividing the total premium (amount over $1,000) by the number of years remaining, i.e., $40 divided by 10, which is $4. So A is $80, less $4 — or $76.

B is the total of the current price of the bond, plus its value at maturity, divided by two. In our example, that will be $1,040, plus $1,000 — or $2,040 — divided by 2, for a figure of $1,020.

If you divide A, which is $76, by B, which is $1,020, you get 7.45 percent. This particular calculation came very close to the actual figure found in a bond basis book of 7.43 percent.

But what if the bond for which you would like to figure out the yield to maturity is selling at a discount instead of at a premium?

All you have to do is make one little change in the formula and everything else works the same. You change the top line of the formula from annual coupon interest, less the total premium, divided by the years remaining to maturity to: annual coupon interest, PLUS the total discount, divided by the remaining years to maturity.

Keep in mind that this formula is only meant to be a quick guide. In general, you will find it most accurate with medium to shorter length maturities and not as accurate with bonds extending out 25 to 30 years. In these latter cases, the variance can be a whole percentage point off if the coupon and effective offering yield are wide apart.

BOND'S CALL FEATURE CAN BE UNFAIR

Many investors holding long-term bonds with very large coupons are surprised to learn that the value of their security is not what they think it should be. They are being rudely introduced to a part of their security they may not have paid much attention to before: The "call" feature.

Very simply, the call provision allows the issuer, whether it is a corporation or a municipality, to call back or redeem the bonds issued before the stated maturity date.

No doubt it does not seem fair to you that, even though you took the risk of buying what you thought was a long-term bond at a time when others were afraid to, your bond can now be called in, forcing you to re-invest the money at a lower yield.

But when interest rates fall dramatically, it happens all over. Those in the popular government funds will find their yields have come down as individuals all across the country re-finance their mortgages at a lower rate.

Corporations that were forced to borrow to keep going at a time when interest rates seemed unbearable, now borrow new money at cheaper rates and call in as much high debt as possible. If your security is called in, you might be angry, but those who work at the company or own shares in the corporation are benefiting with a more financially sound company.

The municipal bond area seems to have more variations of call provisions than any other.

Some calls were set up to be mandatory. That is, if certain factors occur, the issuing municipality or agency must redeem the bonds. For the most part, this is a protection to the investor.

For example, say the project that was financed was destroyed by fire or tornado, or, for other reasons, could not continue to earn the revenues necessary to pay the bond holders and meet the principal payment down the road. You would be happy to have your bonds redeemed and get back the money you invested.

In the case of many high-coupon housing bonds issued at a time of very high interest rates to help raise mortgage money, investors find their bonds called in and their money returned to them because individuals no longer take advantage of the funds raised. With lower interest rates they find they can borrow monies elsewhere at a lower yield.

In some cases, the money raised might have been all let out to homebuyers before interest rates started to fall. Some of these borrowers, however, when rates fall will re-finance their homes; and as these funds come back, the proceeds must be used to retire outstanding bond issues.

But although most municipal bonds do not carry a mandatory call provision, they do often carry an optional call feature that allows the bond to be called in five or 10 years at a price over par.

The premium that is offered the holder of the bond is designed to soften the blow of having the bond called back. Very commonly, it might be three points: 103, with 100 being par. On 10 bonds, you would receive $10,000 plus $300.

Once the call date has come and the issuer has not called in the bond, the bond might be subject to call at any time after that at a steadily declining premium until it reaches callable at par.

Sometimes, two neighbors will have the same bond issue, and one will moan to the other about having his bond called in for redemption. The second neighbor is surprised because they have not have had their bond called.

This is because many times, the calling of bonds is done by random. The names come out of the hat, so to speak.

Of course, there could be another reason our second neighbor was not aware of the bond call.

If that neighbor keeps his or her bonds in a safe deposit vault, and the bond was called right after the last coupon was paid, the neighbor will not find out their bond was called for another six months or more. That means the bond issuer has had free use of their money for at least half a year.

The easy solution to this problem, as we have discussed many times before, is to bring your bonds to a brokerage firm and have them hold your securities. You have insurance protection, and, if your bond is called, you will be notified and the money will be collected for you just as soon as it is paid.

I know. A lot of you just like going to the bank and clipping the coupons. If so, why not consider putting just a few of each issue with the brokerage firm. That way you will be notified if there is a bond call, and you can still keep the bulk of the issue in the vault, where you can clip the coupons.

CHAPTER 18
INCOME STOCKS

WHAT IS YOUR STOCK REALLY YIELDING TODAY?

Someone observed that the only difference between the stock market and the race track is that, in the stock market, if your "horse" is losing, you can always change to another horse.

Unfortunately, the advantage of being able to switch your assets from one to another is ignored by many investors.

Too often, investors tend to marry a stock. They seem to believe they are the only ones holding a particular security, and they do not want to let it down during bad times by selling it and putting their money elsewhere, so they hang in there.

Well, falling in love with your securities is a little like trying to cozy up to a favorite stuffed animal. If you want to do it and it makes you feel better, fine, but the other party couldn't care less.

Then, of course, many people do not consider they have a loss in a particular issue until it is sold. They call it a paper loss, and that way, they think it does not count. Besides, they say, it might be a subject of a takeover down the road. Yes, it could, but so could any number of stocks, and would you buy that same issue today for that reason?

Even those doing very well with certain stocks have trouble sometimes realizing what is fact and what is history.

Take the case of the investor who bought a couple hundred shares of a utility a few of years ago at $18 a share when the dividend was $1.80. He got a yield on his investment of 10 percent.

Now, two years later, the stock is trading at $23 a share and the dividend has been increased to $2 a share.

Many investors will say they have an excellent income stock there. They are getting about 11 percent on their investment. They see it as their original $18 getting them a $2 dividend. That is correct when you look at it mathematically. But how does the portfolio manager or experienced investor see it?

As of this moment, the person has $23 on the table earning a dividend of $2. That is a current return of just over 8.5 percent. Those dollars are not returning what they could if they were somewhere else, in a corporate bond fund, for example, yielding close to 12 percent.

There may be reasons not to sell the original issue and take the profit and re-invest into another income vehicle; but, for the most part, it would make sense to do just that if you want to increase your income. So, when you look over your holdings, look at what they are doing for you today and not what they were doing yesterday.

Of course, there may be times when you want to put off selling an issue because of taxes. But this should be more the exception than the rule.

So many times have I seen a person not wanting to sell an issue that is up perhaps 10 points because he or she does not want to pay the taxes. Some of these people actually seem to feel better when the stock comes back down and has only about a three-point profit in it. It is human nature.

Remember the old adage: Do not cut off your nose to spite your face. Do not be so dead set against paying Uncle Sam a few dollars of taxes that you lose a clear-cut profit. Besides, in many cases, the profit can be offset against some other loss you may have in your portfolio.

So, review your holdings. And when you do, don't just look at the obvious.

CHAPTER 19
GETTING THE DIVIDEND

EX-DIVIDEND DATE IS
KEY TO GETTING DIVIDEND

This is going to be one of those articles you will want to be sure to save for future reference. It could save you dollars and aggravation.

Has it ever happened that you sell a stock, thinking you are going to get one more dividend — and you do — except the brokerage firm calls and says you are not entitled to it — the buyer is due the dividend?

Not a nice surprise.

Of course, it works the other way, too. You hear about a stock paying a dividend along with its regular cash dividend, and you want in. You find out if you buy the stock today you will indeed get the package. However, you discover the next day that the stock has gone down about the same amount as the dividend it paid yesterday.

In working with common stocks and their dividends, there are a few dates you should know; but if you forget them, at least keep the significance of the ex-dividend, or "ex" date in mind.

There is the record date, the ex date and the pay date. Here is how they relate to each other.

Say you are thinking of buying shares of XYZ. Each share pays a quarterly dividend of 55 cents. That works out to $2.20 per year. You like its prospects for continued growth, and you can use the dividend to augment your income.

On July 28 of this year, the company announced it will pay its regular quarterly dividend of 55 cents on September 10 to shareholders of record on August 15.

You want the stock and you want the dividend. Up to what day can you put your order in to purchase the stock and still be sure of collecting the dividend?

The answer is August 8.

You ignore the payment date, because all that tells you is that is when you will get your check. What you want to figure out is when the cutoff will be. That date is called the ex-dividend date. The ex-dividend date is the first day the stock will trade 'ex', i.e., without the dividend.

It is a matter of policy for that date to be almost always the fourth business day preceding the record date.

In our example of XYZ, the record date was announced as August 15. The fourth business day preceding it is August 9. But that is the ex date — the day without the dividend, so you must make your purchase at least one day before.

You can see why you can ignore all the other dates and just know the ex date to make your plans. This is the date that is programmed in the quote machine that your broker uses to instantly tell you whether you will get the dividend.

Naturally, it takes time to process the thousands of shares transferred between buyer and seller each day. That is why sometimes when you sell your stock right before the ex date you get the dividend in the mailbox or credited on your monthly account statement, even though you are not entitled to it. It is simply a case of the company not having time to remove your name from the records and insert the name and address of the new owner.

None of this applies when you buy or sell corporate or tax-free municipal bonds.

Bonds pay interest every six months. But there is no special date that determines whether you get the full six months' interest. When the interest is paid, you are entitled to a pro rata share for each day you owned the bond. So, in essence, it makes no difference with regard to interest when you sell the bond.

The person buying your bond would pay you the bond's price plus the accrued interest you earned. Then, when the bond paid the full six months' interest, the new owner would simply keep the whole thing.

In all of these examples, it is the trade date that counts. That is the date you bought or sold the security.

The settlement date is when you deliver either the cash or the securities to the firm. With common stock, it is usually five business days. With bonds, especially those purchased on a new offering, settlement might be several weeks away. Be sure to check your trade confirmation slip for the date. No use giving someone else the float on your money.

Keep in mind that you are responsible for making good the payment of either cash or securities on settlement date. If you are late in making payment because you have not received the confirmation slip, you will usually be charged interest for each day of delay.

CHAPTER 20
THE DOW INDEX

HOW THE DOW JONES CAME TO BE

So often people will ask a broker what the Dow is doing or what it closed at. The broker will usually say "Up 3 points," or whatever.

The investor, or would-be investor, walks away thinking he has a general feeling of how the market was performing.

The fact is, the Dow Jones Industrial Average is not always a very accurate barometer of what the overall market is doing.

Over the years, it is not uncommon for one of the Dow stocks to suffer a major drop, or spike up, of a dozen points or more in a day. These unusual and large swings throw the Dow Jones Average down, or up, much further than what the market generally warranted.

If you happen to be one of the millions of viewers of the evening news that same week and were not following the market too closely, you could see an exaggerated drop in the Dow Jones Industrial Average.

A more accurate picture of the market can be gotten by following some of the newer indexes, such as the Standard and Poor's 500. Another good gauge is looking at the ending market, that is, how many issues are up and how many are down at any given moment.

The make-up of the Dow averages actually goes back to 1884, according to information included in a newsletter recently published by the Hartford Insurance group.

The article retells the story of how financial publisher Charles Henry Dow and his associates, Edwin Davis Jones and Charles Bergstresser, became known as Dow, Jones, & Co.

Mr. Dow wanted to provide investors with an indicator of the general stock market conditions. He selected nine of the strong railroad companies and added two other industrial companies, then divided their combined stock prices by 11 to arrive at his average.

As the story goes, this information was published each day in his newsletter called "Customer's Afternoon Letter," which later evolved into the *Wall Street Journal*.

Over the years, the average was expanded into three separate averages. One for industrials, another for utilities and a third for transportation companies. Today, there are 30 companies in the first, 15 in the second, and 20 in the last grouping.

During the first 50 years or so, there were a reported 100 or so additions and deletions from the Industrial Average. However, in the last half century, there have been less than a dozen changes.

In 1975, Minnesota Mining and Manufacturing was added. In 1979, the big drug concern Merck was added, as well as the dominant member today, IBM. Finally, a couple of years ago, Manville Company was dropped and replaced by American Express.

For all of its abuse by many professionals, the Dow Jones is still the most recognized of indexes. Mr. Dow's objective of providing us with a quick reference point to the direction of the economy has been pretty accurate over the years.

According to Dow, a bull market is on the rise when the average sets new highs, then briefly retreats, and subsequently pushes higher. Conversely, a bear market exists when we have successive lows.

CHAPTER 21
ENTERING ORDERS

CORRECT USE OF STOPS, LIMIT AND MARKET ORDERS

Knowing how to put in the right order to buy or sell your stocks can be extremely important to the final outcome.

For example, you have just heard on the radio the stock market is reacting very negatively to a new economic report released. While you are not worried about most of your holdings, there is one issue in which you have a big gain and do not want to see it disappear.

You get to a telephone and anxiously ask your broker for the latest quote on XYZ. He or she tells you the Dow Jones is down 43 points and your XYZ is down 2 points.

Your broker tells you that while the market is still falling quickly, some analysts believe the market has overreacted and will rebound before the day is over.

What to do?

Here is where knowing the differences between a market order, a stop order and a stop limit order can be vitally important.

The market order is the usual order given in cases like this. It will get you out as soon as the order hits the trading floor. Unfortunately, because the market is moving so quickly, you cannot be sure what you will end up getting for your stock. It could be several points lower. And what if the market does rebound just after your order goes off? You could end up with the low for the day only to see the market rebound and your stock end up a couple of points higher on the day.

A second option would be a stop order to sell at a price you select. It works like this.

You would instruct your broker to put an order in to sell your stock with a stop at say 25. This means if the market for your stock continues to fall and reaches 25, your order is triggered and becomes a market order ready to go off on the next trade.

Usually, this means you will get your 25 or some price very close to it. However, at times of unusual activity, it is possible your stock may be falling in chunks or gaps, and the next trade could be a couple or even several points away from the stop price you selected.

It is just this type of situation that often leads to misunderstandings when you are informed you did sell your stock, but at a price way below what you expected.

To protect something like that from happening in a fast-moving market, you can employ what is called a stop limit order.

This order works like the prior stop order; that is, it is activated when your stock trades at the price you put the stop in at. Only in this case, when a subsequent trade is made, it must be at the price of your order or better.

This can be particularly useful when there might be big gaps between trades, and you do not want to risk selling way below your stop price.

For example, XYZ is at 58 and you are worried it might fall on some pending news. You put in a stop limit order to sell XYZ at stop 52 — limit 51. Subsequently, news is released that is quite damaging and XYZ plunges. It falls to 52 and your stop order is activated. However, the next trade is going to be at 50 as the falling pace quickens. In this case, you would not sell your stock. You had attached a limit of 51, meaning you would sell only if you would get the 51, or better, and that is not possible as the next trade is going to be at 50.

The key to keep in mind is while the stop order and the stop limit order offer you some protection, they each have a weakness.

In the case of the stop order, it does not guarantee an execution at your stated price; and the stop limit order does not guarantee that you will have an execution at all. In our example, the market could continue to fall after triggering your stop limit order. So, if you need to get out and want to be sure, the market order still makes a lot of sense.

SECTION THREE:
YOUR INVESTMENT CHOICES

CHAPTER 22
OPTIONS

OPTION WRITING INVOLVES TWO KINDS OF RISK

Option writing is a recognized way to increase income without locking up money into fixed long-term vehicles.

Because option writing is not widely understood by investors, let's talk about it further and run through an example of an option writing transaction. This will perhaps uncover some of the mystery.

Let us say you believe the stock market will work its way higher during the year. However, you are not as interested in making capital gains as you are in increasing your income. Your money market funds are now paying a lot less than they did a few years ago, and the local bank certificates of deposit are pretty low as well.

You feel you need higher yields on your money. Yet, whether right or wrong, you have decided not to lock up any more money into long-term investments, because you are afraid of interest rates rising in the future.

New Motor Company is a stock you believe will do well. It has been trading between $23 and $45 but is currently selling for 42 1/4. It pays a dividend of 60 cents quarterly. You like the market and this stock. You believe the stock will probably sell for over $45 a share by the end of the year.

Here is how it would look if you decided to purchase 200 shares of the stock and at the same time sell or write an option to give up the stock anytime between now and the third Friday of December (that's about eight months from now) for $45 a share.

On the negative side, your costs will be the price of 200 shares, plus the commission. Also, you will pay a commission to sell the option on the stock. If your shares of New Motor are indeed called away in December, because the stock has gone over your option price, you will pay another commission to sell your stock.

On the other side of the ledger, here is what you stand to gain.

You purchase the stock at $42.25 and sell it for $45, which was the option strike price, making $2.75 on each share. While you owned the stock between now and the third Friday of December, you received two quarterly dividends. That's another $1.20 per share. You also keep the option premium money you got when you first sold the option. In this example, it was $2.45 a share.

Using a computer program, I can tell you, if you made this trade, and in December, New Motor was called away from you, you would, after all commissions, have netted 13 percent on your investment.

Now remember, that is for about eight months. If you annualize your investment to compare it to other investments, your return would come out to 19 percent. By the way, those commissions were standard prices. If you did the trades for less, your return would be higher.

A nice return, no doubt, but let us look at the two basic risks you must weigh.

One is real and the other is, what I term, psychological. Let's take the latter first.

Say you were more than right in your expectations of what the market and New Motor were going to do during the rest of the year. You have come away with a very nice return on your money. However, if New Motor zoomed up to $60 a share, you could easily get down on yourself for having to let it go at $45. You know, you finally had a winner and you had to give it up.

Actually, there are ways to close out your position early and keep the stock if you see that it is running, but that is starting to get into too much detail. If you really want to do this, you should read more on the topic and sit down with someone who does a lot of option writing.

The other risk is real. You are still dealing with securities. You purchased New Motor for $42.25 and immediately took in $2.45 for selling your option, reducing your cost to about $39.80. But if New Motor falls to $35, you still have a loss.

This is where the mutual fund approach to option writing has the advantage of spreading out the risk. These funds are working with scores of trades at all times, rather than just one or two. The funds can also work strategies anticipating a drop in a stock and employing the overall market options.

OPTION WRITING FOR INCOME

More and more, I am seeing investors come to grips with the fact that their money market accounts are not earning enough to give them the returns they want. And they are wondering where they should go now.

History tells us to be careful about rushing out and locking up those high yields in long-term bonds. We learned when interest rates start moving higher, those dollars can be eroded away very quickly.

But then again, maybe rates will not turn up so soon and that is the best plan to follow right now. But, if you have doubt and you are looking for an alternative, you could consider option writing.

It is a shame that option writing's half brother, option buying, has stolen the option spotlight, because it is so much flashier. Unfortunately, there are so many stories told about people playing around with option buying and getting hurt that as soon as a stockbroker or other financial adviser tries to introduce the other side of the option family, option writing, people tend to turn away thinking the two are similar.

In fact, the two could not be more different.

While option buying can be described as similar to gambling in Las Vegas — you know, you can win big, but if you stick around and keep playing, you will eventually give it all back to the house. Option writing is safe enough for pension plans, IRA accounts and the fictitious little widowed lady the Securities and Exchange Commission seeks to protect.

And more and more people have been discovering option writing as a method of gaining attractive income, while not having to lock their money up in a fixed-rate investment for 20 to 30 years.

Option writing can be described as being relatively conservative, certainly more conservative than owning a portfolio of stock like General Motors, American Telephone, IBM and General Electric. Because, in an option writing program, you actually own those stocks like another investor might, only you have written an option on them allowing someone else to buy them from you at a stated price some time down the road.

The investor that buys the options on your stock is on the high-leveraged, high-risk end of the transaction. He or she has the potential to win big or lose big. You, as the person that sold the options, have chosen to give up some potential upside movement in those stocks for some immediate cash in your pocket.

You also get to keep any dividends the stocks pay while you own them and, if your stock is called from you, there can be additional dollars from appreciation as well.

You can buy individual stocks and write options on them, and many people do this with the aid of a computer program to help them figure out their returns ahead of time. But, chances are, if you have little experience in the market or little time for trading individual issues, you will be better off in one of the several option writing income mutual funds.

Because options are somewhat complicated, before starting on your own or investing in a mutual fund, be sure you read over the booklet, *Understanding Options*, available at any brokerage firm, or the fund prospectus.

CHAPTER 23
MUTUAL FUNDS

SPECIAL FUNDS FOR FOREIGN INVESTORS

Throughout the year, we see many visitors from areas like South America, Canada, Europe and the Pacific.

Many of these people have been coming year after year, and many of them over the years have brought money into the country. They like the safety and stability of America.

But while the really big money has specially trained money managers seeking out the best vehicles to earn top interest, the individual non-resident alien has not always understood where he or she can go for a better potential return on their money.

The majority of foreign visitors choose to invest their dollars in America in a way that will not subject them to oftentimes having as much as 30 percent of the earnings withheld for taxes. The reason, of course, is while they can get a credit for the amount withheld, it usually means filing a return with their own country; and that is something they would prefer not to do for one reason or another.

So the majority of non-resident aliens have mostly stuck to bank saving accounts, certificates of deposit or certain insurance policies paying interest. The U. S. government does not withhold any taxes from these earnings.

But what many non-resident aliens are not aware of, is since the passage of the Deficit Reduction Act in 1984, virtually all corporate and government bonds issued after July, 1984, now also are exempt from the withholding requirements.

The significance is that while the value of these securities will fluctuate with the movement of interest rates, they are considered appropriate for the conservative investor, and they do pay higher yields. Usually one to three percent over the prime interest rate. And when you remember the income from these debt instruments is not subject to any withholding taxes for the non-resident alien, that means it is a pure profit.

The laws in this area, defining who is and who is not an alien, or a resident alien versus a non-resident alien, are such that you should really talk it over with your tax advisor. But generally a person is considered a non-resident alien if they are visiting in this country for fewer than 31 days during the year, or, using a somewhat complicated average system, over the last three years they are present on fewer than 122 days a year.

Now if you or someone you know falls into the category of non-resident alien and you would like to increase the return potential of your money in the United States, there are some specially designed funds that will make it a lot easier for you to put your money to work.

These funds allow you to direct your dollars into a portfolio of approved government issues or qualifying corporate bonds. If you want absolutely no fluctuation on your invested dollar and are willing to earn less, you can place your money in a money market account. You can even switch it from one position to another as you or your financial advisor see fit.

Investors in the funds can order checks on their

account so they can redeem shares by check. This way they can make withdrawals as they see fit or even pay bills they accumulate in America with U. S. dollars. They can even arrange to have money wired directly from the fund into a bank account they keep in the United States. Some like to do this just before they know they are going to be coming for a visit.

If you do choose to invest your dollars through a fund, remember mutual funds are sold by prospectus only, and you should read it carefully before you invest or send any money.

GET THE RIGHT MONEY MARKET FUND

Even though money market mutual funds have been around for about a decade, there are still millions of Americans that are missing this simple way to increase the rate of return on their savings.

Money market mutual funds consistently pay more than the prime interest rate.

In addition to this attractive yield, they offer safety and daily liquidity to big and small investor alike.

When money market mutual funds first appeared in the late 70s, they were used mostly by investors to park money between stock market trades.

However, when inflation and interest rates went sky-high in 1980 and 1981, many Americans who did not know the first thing about either stocks or bonds, learned they could use the money market funds managed by mutual fund companies to have their money earn the same high yields enjoyed by mega-buck investors. The funds were paying as much as 16 percent.

Shortly thereafter, interest rates started to decline and banks introduced their money funds in an effort to gain back their lost depositors. To entice them back, many of the financial institutions paid an interest rate above what the money market mutual funds were paying. Banks, you see, unlike money market mutual funds which pay out what they can earn, can pay whatever rate they decide. Lately, that has meant a good one percent less than the mutual fund money market accounts.

Today, there are more than 300 different money market accounts. Some are for those wanting tax free income only, some manage only government securities in the fund, but most are made up of very short-term safe investments such as short-term bank CDs, U.S. government treasuries and prime commercial paper. These are IOUs between major corporations, for several days or several weeks, and in sizes the average person cannot deal with.

So when you hear a question as to how safe is your money in a money market mutual fund, the answer, I believe, is very safe.

How easy is it to get my money out?

Money funds are very liquid. You can put your money in one day and take it out the next. If you like you can have free checks so you can withdraw the money or you can do like most people and simply telephone the fund or the broker handling your account, and have them sell as many shares as dollars you want. You can even arrange to have the fund wire money to your bank.

Is there a cost?

There is no cost to open an account or to close one out. There is no cost when you deposit money and no cost when you make withdrawals.

How do you go about opening an account?

The simplest personal way is to contact a brokerage firm and open an account through them. All you do is sign a couple of forms and deposit your money. If you like, you can contact any number of mutual fund companies directly and have them send you a prospectus and forms to sign. Sign the forms, send a check, and you are all set.

Can I have a money market account if I only have a small amount of money?

While most brokerage firms put minimums of $5,000 on their money market mutual funds, there are many funds that will let you start with $500 or less.

If you would like additional information on money market mutual funds or an annual guide including addresses and toll-free telephone numbers, write to the Investment Company Institute at 1600 M Street, N.W., Suite 600, Washington, D. C. 20036.

CHAPTER 24
LIMITED PARTNERSHIPS

INFLATION FEARS ANSWERED WITH REAL ESTATE

There are all kinds of studies that prove how great real estate ownership is in building up your net worth.

This is one reason why, over the years, many financial planners have relied on real estate limited partnerships to add diversification to portfolios that would otherwise not be able to participate in real estate.

Most people cannot go out and buy an apartment building or shopping center, because they do not have the capital or the time to manage it. That is where a real estate limited partnership comes in. It allows you to invest just the right amount of dollars to balance your portfolio.

But with so many different partnerships being offered, you need to look closely at the differences between them to find the one that will provide the buying power protection you want.

Here are the features you should have in your partnership if you are looking for income and safety:

#1) Income of about 10 percent, typically paid on a quarterly basis. A number of programs will shelter about a quarter to a third of the income from current taxes so your real rate of return is actually a little higher.

#2) No leverage. When the properties are purchased with cash, there is no mortgage to worry about in bad times.

#3) Existing properties that are already occupied with triple-net leases. A triple-net lease means all operating expenses on the properties, such as maintenance, taxes and insurance, are the responsibility of the tenant.

#4) Insurance on the leases, so in the event a tenant has a bad month or quarter, the insurance company pays the majority of the lost lease income to the partnership for some predetermined period of time.

Before we talk about the partnership's one disadvantage, keep in mind that, while we are happy to accept the nice income it produces, our main purpose is to protect our buying power down the road. That means we expect to sell the real estate for more than what we paid for it. And, to help make the real estate more valuable, the partnership negotiates leases that provide for increases in the rents that are tied to the rising cost of living.

Now for the most commonly cited drawback to real estate limited partnerships: the lack of liquidity.

At least one partnership has found an interesting way to at least provide a degree of liquidity. Its managers have made arrangements with a bank so you can put up your units as collateral for a loan, with no principle payments due until the real estate partnership starts to sell off the properties.

But fundamentally you should be considering real estate as a several-year investment. Think of it this way: If five to seven years of rising interest rates and inflation have caused your bonds to be worth less than what you invested, the same forces should have made your investment in real estate worth more. Match your gains against your losses, and you are whole again.

EQUIPMENT LEASING CAN PRODUCE HIGH YIELD

It is hard to find investments offering yields in the double digits these days. There are some, of course, but you probably will have to make some trade-offs in the area of liquidity, marketability and risk to get them.

Judging from the growing interest in equipment leasing programs, investors are saying they are prepared to do this, at least with some of their money.

Equipment-leasing programs in the form of limited partnerships have been around for more than a decade. They commonly have offered returns over 12 percent and pay monthly. With long-term treasuries a couple of points below, you owe it to yourself to decide whether you can live with the reasons leasing partnerships can promise such high yields.

You need to consider two basic factors. First, it is a partnership. Therefore, it does not have daily marketability. Also, your dollars are in a non-guaranteed investment.

Let us take a closer look at these two potential handicaps and see whether these rule out this investment for you or whether you can tolerate them.

The partnerships are designed to run for about seven to nine years. If you want to come out of the partnership before then, like any other limited partnership, you have to find another buyer. There is no daily market. You should plan on the dollars you put into this investment being there for a while. But with its high stream of cash return, you really should not need to come out of the investment early, if you have diversified the rest of your holdings.

As we have often pointed out, a treasury bond is marketable every day. But, depending on interest rate movements, you may or may not get back all you invested when you sell.

The second thing to look at is the safety of your invested dollars.

Unlike an investment in bonds, which have an interest rate risk, the major risk in equipment leasing is a business risk.

To minimize the risk, many companies putting partnerships together are careful to purchase the equipment and lease it out only after they have a signed agreement with the lessee ahead of time. They are not just going out and buying a whole bunch of equipment and then running around trying to find someone to lease it from them. The arrangement has already been made.

Some of the leases are for three or four years only. Because there is not a guarantee that the equipment will be re-leased a second time, the partnership charges more for these short leases called operating leases.

Other leases, called full pay-out leases, are put into the portfolios to balance the partnership. These leases collect enough payments over the length of the lease to cover the cost of the equipment completely.

The partnerships are also diversified as to the type of equipment owned. Generally, the equipment is computers, printers, telephone equipment and peripheral pieces.

People sometimes make a snap judgment and decide that equipment like that is going to get outdated very rapidly. Changes are happening fast, that's for sure. But remember, most of this equipment has a functioning life of more than 10 years, and even though some companies may need and be able to afford the latest equipment, many smaller companies are only too happy to get something not so new at a bargain price.

In some cases, the present equipment actually holds all its value, because the newer equipment out is so much more expensive. Nevertheless, this is a factor in determining your total return from your investment, and most good partnerships take two other steps to protect your investment.

In the early years, while the partnership is paying you that high interest, it is holding out another couple of percent to purchase additional equipment for the portfolio for the first several years. This builds up the total size of the portfolio beyond what your original dollars bought.

And secondly, the general partner has to be conservative in his estimate of the residual value that will be there when he starts liquidating all of the portfolio in the last couple of years.

CHAPTER 25
BONDS

PREMIUM BONDS OFTEN YOUR BEST BUY

If you were in the market to purchase some tax-free municipal bonds and you were offered two issues — an 8 3/4 bond priced at $1,064 to yield 7.4 percent for six years, or a 7.4 bond at par, would you automatically find yourself taking the par bond?

If you are like most investors, you would.

Maybe it is because it is easier to figure your return on invested dollars by working with par bonds only, or maybe it is because you do not like the idea of entering into a transaction where you know right from the start you are not going to get all of your principal back.

For our readers who may not be familiar with bond terminology, a bond selling at par sells for $1,000 for $1,000 face value. A premium bond would sell for some amount over $1,000, and at maturity, you would receive only the face value of the bond ($1,000) — not what you paid for it.

In any event, ask any bond trader, and he will tell you that bonds selling at par, that is $1,000, are a lot easier to sell than bonds selling at a premium. In fact, many investors are insulted that their broker would even show them a premium bond.

But using the above example, I want to show you how sometimes your best purchase can be a premium bond.

First, let us start with the easy part. The bond with the larger coupon rate of 8 3/4 is naturally going to pay you a larger check every six months than the bond with the 7.4 percent yield. And no one is going to argue with receiving more tax-free income.

But what about that terrible premium you had to pay to get that larger check?

Let us take a look and see just how terrible it really is. I think you are going to find that sometimes it is more psychological than real.

In our example, let's say you actually paid $64.50 over par for each bond. If you figure the bond has a six-year life to maturity, you would spread out your loss of $64.50 over the six years. That would amount to $10.75 per year.

But look! Your premium bond is paying you $13.50 more than the par bond. The premium bond is paying $87.50 per year and the par bond is paying $74. Therefore, you can recoup your loss each year you amortize the premium and still be ahead.

In this example, it would be $87.50 per year, minus the yearly premium amount of $10.75, equaling $76.75. That is still more than the par bond at 7.4 percent, yielding $74.

It may seem like a small amount, but then you are talking about many bonds, not just one, and, also, we did not say the premium bond would give you a big killing over the par bond, just that it will often hold its own and you should not immediately turn down a good quality bond selling at a premium.

CHAPTER 26
GNMA

GINNIE MAE CAN BE A HEARTBREAKER

Ah, Ginnie Mae, you are so enticing. With all of your many attributes, you seem to guarantee happiness for those that turn to you. And yet, with few exceptions, you have left a trail of broken hearts and purses.

Maybe a little dramatic, but the sad fact is there is a lot of truth to the above.

Ask most investors who have purchased a Ginnie Mae certificate, and they will tell you they liked the high yield, the government guarantee of interest and principal and the rather short average life of the investment.

These are likable features if ever we saw them. The problem is, GNMAs, or Government National Mortgage Association certificates, although similar, do not work exactly like corporate bonds.

With GNMAs, if you purchase a certificate paying say 11 percent, you have just bought a pool of mortgages that theoretically run for 30 years. However, as you should know from your own experience, few people today stay in the same house for 30 years. As a result, these mortgages are paid off early.

As people retire the mortgages in your pool, you are given back some of your principal each month, and eventually, all of your invested money will be returned. In fact, the U. S. government guarantees you this.

At first glance, this looks like a great feature. And in times of rising interest rates, it is. But other times, it can work against you.

For example, you purchase a GNMA pool yielding 11 percent because you believe interest rates are not liable to go much higher, and in fact, may fall in the future.

Let us say you are right: interest rates soon fall to 9 percent levels. You are sitting back, thinking you have invested your money at the higher rates and will enjoy the higher returns.

But remember, we said each month some principal is being returned to you as various people pay off their mortgages. And if interest rates fall, you will usually find more people will get out of those higher mortgages; and you, dear investor, will find your principal will be coming back to you in bigger chunks that you would like. In other words, less and less of your original invested dollars will be earning the 11 percent.

Conversely, you purchase your GNMA yielding 11 percent, and interest rates move dramatically up to 14 percent. Now you are thinking how glad you are you have purchased a GNMA certificate, because, as the monthly checks come in with some of your principal being returned to you, you will be able to reinvest these dollars into higher yielding investments.

But now people are not in a hurry to pay off their low mortgages to assume higher ones. As a result, you will probably see very little principal come back to you each month.

In other words, when you do not want to see much of your principal come back, it tends to come back in globs. When you would love to get your principal back quickly, it dribbles back to you.

Someone might say there is nothing to be too concerned about, because even if interest rates go against you, your GNMA pool has an average life of only 12 years. This one is a little tricky, too.

If you are told GNMAs have an average life of 12 years, you might presume that some pools pay back all their principal in 8 to 10 years and some 12 to 14 years with the average being 12 years.

But, that is not what they mean when they say the average life of a GNMA pool is 12 years.

Average life is used to describe that point when experience says that half of the 30 year mortgages in a typical pool will have been paid back. It is saying, based on the history of pay-backs in this pool, this will be the average number of years each principal dollar will be outstanding. It does not mean your pool will have paid back all of its principal to you in a dozen years.

LITTLE KNOWN CMOs HAVE TERRIFIC FEATURES

If you are looking for income but are concerned about safety, here is a little-known investment idea.

This investment pays you a rate of interest equal to long-term U. S. treasury bonds, is government guaranteed, and can be sold at any time in the marketplace or, and here is the key, can be "put", that is, returned to the trustee for your money back.

We are talking about collateralized mortgage obligations bonds that are secured 100 percent by GNMA government guaranteed mortgages.

While similar to regular GNMA pools, it is the "put" feature of these pools that gives them a unique advantage and has a growing number of investors snapping up more and more.

Let us back up a little to explain an important difference between these pools.

In a regular GNMA pool, the investor buys a share, usually in $25,000 size, of a large assortment of mortgages. Each month the investor receives a check made up of interest on his or her investment plus some of the principal. The principal is the investor's own money coming back as mortgages in the pool are paid back.

While most mortgages are for 30 years, all you have to do is look at your own situation or that of any number of your friends to realize Americans move around so often. Most of the mortgages end up lasting for a much shorter time.

However, these collateralized mortgage obligation pools, or CMOs, differ from the regular ones in they are almost completely made up of mortgages on low-end starter homes. That means the mortgages in these pools should be paid off much faster than standard pools.

Why?

Because these buyers are going to be more transient. They start a family and need to move to a bigger house. There is a job promotion and they want to buy a larger house, or perhaps there is a job transfer, and they have to move. Keep in mind the government guarantees these mortgages, so you do not have a credit risk with these home owners.

While there is really no way of knowing for sure how fast these mortgages will turn over, to me it makes sense to think that after two or three years, there will be a lot of mortgages being paid off.

But wait, the real unique characteristic of these pools is their "put" feature. It gives you another way out. Besides, you have a marketplace, should interest rates go against you after you have invested your money.

Think of it as an investment having two separate pay windows. For regular interest and a little principal coming each month, you stand in line A. That is the way a typical GNMA pool works, although, even in this case, your money should come back faster. These mortgages are on starter homes, remember.

But if you want out sooner, you get in line B. This line is for those wanting to get their principal as quickly as possible.

All regular payments of principal and any prepayments from the mortgages go to a special escrowed redemption fund used to pay those investors standing in line B before any money goes to those in line A. It stands to reason, then, that if you are in that line, you could expect to get most, or possibly all, of your principal back within several years.

Because there are a number of variations with these CMO bonds, if this seems like something that could be useful to you, try contacting your investment advisor for a booklet that will explain it in greater detail.

CHAPTER 27
TAX FREE

THREE LETTERS — AMT — CAN SPELL HIGHER YIELDS FOR YOU

People still seem to be confused about which municipal tax-free bonds are safe and which ones will end up taxable.

Just recently, I overheard a broker on the telephone telling someone about an attractive new issue of tax-free bonds that was paying 7 1/2 percent. From the conversation, I could guess the party on the other end was questioning why this particular bond was paying about half a percent more than most current bonds.

The broker was trying to explain that, because the bond will have its income classed as a preference item (which means it could end up being taxable to some people), the bond issue had to come out a little richer. That is bond talk for a little higher.

The person at the other end of the line either did not understand the importance of a bond being subject to the alternative minimum tax, or he or she did not know whether this bond would be vulnerable to the tax.

If you are still a buyer of individual issues, you really need to stop and figure out whether you will have AMT exposure or not. This way, when you get a call about one of these bonds, you will know whether you should take advantage of their high yield or stay away.

You really need to discuss this matter with your tax adviser, but let us cover the key elements to see whether we can put you at ease.

Paying your tax based on the regular computation or the alternative minimum tax computation has been going on for years. It is just that in the past, most people paid their taxes based on the regular method. You did not hear much about the alternative minimum tax.

But, the tax reform act of 1986 made a few changes. Still, to even begin to be subject to this alternative minimum tax, you would need to have a lot of exposure by having: 1) received income from private activity bonds issued on or after August 8, 1986; 2) had gains on the exercise of incentive stock options; 3) donated a large amount of capital to a charity with a build-up of capital gains in it; or 4) have outstanding tax shelters.

If you are involved in one of these areas, it still does not necessarily mean you will have to pay the minimum tax. But, you might want to do some rough figuring.

Start with your adjusted gross income. That is usually the figure at the bottom of the first page on your 1040. It is all your income, minus certain deductions, such as your Keogh deductions, alimony payment and moving expenses.

Now, add in any preference items.

. Subtract deductions for charitable contributions, medical and casualty losses exceeding 10 percent of your adjusted gross income, real estate taxes and interest expenses not in excess of your investment income.

This gives you your alternative minimum tax base.

From this figure, subtract $40,000, if you file a joint return, or $30,000 if you file a single return. (There is a phase-out of this amount, but for rough figuring, I am going to ignore it.) What is left is your alternative minimum taxable income.

If paying tax on that amount at 21 percent is greater than the tax you would pay, figuring your tax the regular way, then you have to pay this amount.

You then can tell people you are subject to the alternative minimum tax.

What are your chances of falling subject to AMT?
Fortunately, not very high.

For example, a person with an alternative minimum tax base of $75,000 could have as much as $400,000 of those 7 1/2 percent tax-free bonds the broker was calling about, if they had no other preference income. If your AMT base ends up being $150,000, you could buy about $650,000 of those bonds.

That is because, again figuring it roughly, if you had taxable income of $50,000, whether you filed singularly or jointly, you could have preference income of about $40,000 and still not be subject to the alternative minimum tax.

CHAPTER 28
UNIT TRUSTS

UNIT TRUSTS MAKE
CONVENIENT PACKAGE

If you purchased any of your stocks or bonds in 1988 in the form of a unit trust, you certainly were not alone.

Figures just released by the Investment Company Institute show altogether investors purchased $12.7 billion of various unit trusts during 1988.

It was not too long ago unit trusts were mostly used to bundle a large number of bonds, maybe as many as 60 different issues, into a package. Then the package was divided into separate units, usually $1,000 each. An owner of one unit actually owned a small percent of each and every bond. It was another way investors could get diversification with just a small investment.

But today you can find a seemingly endless variety of securities packaged as a unit trust.

Take tax-free bonds as an example. You can get unit trusts for long-term, short-term and medium-term bonds. They can be insured or not insured. They can be just Florida bonds or from all over the country. You get the idea.

The same is true for corporate and government issues. There are even unit trusts for various groupings of common stock.

The most popular packages in 1988?

Unit trusts of tax-free bonds totaled $8 billion. Corporate, government and other taxable debt instruments amounted to $3 billion. And the amount of equities purchased through a unit trust rounded out the figures at $1.7 billion. Figures for 1989 look about the same.

Why are unit trusts so popular with many investors?

Well, one thing is the way you can get a great deal of diversification with a small investment.

For people looking for income from their investments, unit trusts are a treat because rather than pay interest every quarter like a stock or every six months like an individual bond, you can get your interest monthly if you desire.

Unit trusts are not immune to price fluctuations due to rising or falling interest rates or a rising or falling Dow Jones. But rather than paying for ongoing management to continually massage the portfolio during these ups and downs, investors in a unit trust know if they stay put eventually each bond in their portfolio will mature at its face value.

Unit trusts are quoted daily based on the value of each and every holding within the trusts. Generally, the price you pay when purchasing a unit trusts includes a commission. There is usually no commission added in when you sell.

Before making a purchase of a unit trust, it is a good idea to read the prospectus.

CHAPTER 29
ZERO-COUPON

ZERO-COUPON SECURITIES NOT ENTIRELY RISK FREE

Let us discuss zero-coupon treasury bonds, generally considered to be among the safest of investments . . . but where the risk may be lying in wait.

The concept of zero-coupons is taking a fixed security, like a corporate bond or government treasury bond, and physically stripping from it all of its future coupon payments.

It would be like taking an ear of corn and stripping off all of the kernels. You would be left with the cob, which would be similar to our principal bond in this case, and a pile of kernels, representing a whole lot of six-month payments.

The underlying security is then offered for sale at a price less than its face or maturity value. It sells for less than face value, because the buyer is buying the security without any six-month coupons of interest payments attached.

And if you think buying a bond without any interest coupons seems strange, consider, if you did purchase this bond, each year on your income tax statement you would have to show that you did receive some interest that year, even though you did not.

You can reread the above paragraphs all you want, but it is going to come out the same way. Someone buying a zero-coupon treasury certificate purchases a security at a discount from face value. They receive no interest during the time they hold it, but have to show interest was received, when filing their income tax.

Why would anyone want to purchase such a thing?

First, in the case of the treasury, your underlying security is backed by the federal government, and that is about as safe as you can pragmatically get.

Second, because you are not receiving an interest payment every six months, you do not have to be concerned at what rate of interest you will be re-investing those dollars at over the next number of years.

You do not risk having to re-invest at a lower rate. All the interest is earned at the original rate over the life of the zero-coupon certificate. Your total return is the difference between the price you pay and the maturity value.

Zero-coupon instruments give the investor a sure way of knowing exactly how much a certain sum of money will be worth in a given number of years.

This means, for example, it is possible for someone to purchase these zero-coupon treasuries and know without a doubt how much will be in his or her retirement plan at retirement.

A couple could open a Uniform Transfers To Minors Account and fund it with purchases of these bonds knowing exactly how much will be there down the road to pay for college.

Trading is usually done in units of $1,000 face value. Of course, you can always buy more than one stripped bond. Maturities are usually available from as short as a couple years out to 20 or more years.

When you call your broker to investigate what is available, you will get a quote something like this: "I can sell you a zero bond maturing at $1,000 on November 15, 1999, for $360. Your yield to maturity is 9.2 percent."

An example of a shorter-term zero-coupon bond might be an issue maturing May 15, 1992, that can be purchased for $720 to be worth $1,000 on that date.

You should notice the further out you go, the less money you will have to put up to purchase your unit.

Simple enough. But what about the potential risk or weakness we believe every investment has?

In this case, we have a principal backed by the federal government and a predetermined interest rate not only on the original coupons that came with the bond but with their reinvestment as well.

The risk or weakness is the fact you have locked up your money at a fixed rate of return that looks attractive today. However, if the cost of living, the consumer price index, the prime interest rate and inflation move up, even a modest amount, your money at maturity would not have the same buying power.

Also, while you are assured of your money at maturity, should you in the meantime decide to sell your zero-coupon certificates, you will be doing so subject to the market. You may sell them for a profit, the same price, or a loss, depending on what interest rates have done.

CHAPTER 30
COMMODITIES

TRADING IN COMMODITIES WITH LESS RISK

It was a cool Saturday morning, and it was still early enough to get over to the Coffee Roaster before it got crowded.

As I rounded the parking lot, I could smell the strong aroma of coffee roasting. It reminded me of being back in the old Italian section of San Francisco, more than a decade ago, walking along the North Beach section on one of those unusual sunny days.

Inside were the ever-present sacks of various coffees, and as I passed by on my way to a little table by the corner, I picked up a leaflet on the counter telling all about coffee, from the bean to the cup. However, the leaflet failed to mention that coffee is one of the most actively traded commodities. And people have made a lot of money trading coffee futures.

It got me to thinking that maybe it was time we took another look at commodities, or futures as they like to be called now, as an investment vehicle.

There is an old joke that says if ever you are on a flight and you want to get some work done or catch some sleep and the person beside you keeps wanting to talk, you should ask them what they do for a living. When the person asks you, tell them you sell life insurance.

Well, the same thing can probably be said about beginning a conversation on investing by talking about trading commodities.

Let's face it. Most people still view trading commodities the way it was depicted in the movie, *Trading Places*, where fortunes were made and lost in minutes. Many consider it akin to rolling the dice at the Golden Nugget, and perhaps not nearly as much fun.

And yet, many of these people call their broker and want to buy all they can of an obscure $2 stock because they were told by a friend that something was supposed to happen.

The fact is, a growing number of investors are discovering that trading futures through a quasi mutual fund/limited partnership, can be very satisfying.

Wall Street seems to have been able to tame down futures trading so the average investor can get involved with less money and less risk. You can get into these new pools with as little as $5,000 to $10,000 and never receive a margin call for more money. In fact, commodities have been approved for IRA investments, and, in this case, you can invest as little as $2,000.

Many people know commodities were the place to be during the late 70s and early 80s while inflation was running high. Then, the following couple of years saw low inflation, and for the most part, lower profits for commodity traders.

And yet, in the last couple of years, with inflation at its lowest point in years, many of these commodity funds did well. Why?

Today's commodity funds are trading much of their money in financial futures and stock indexes. Sure, they are still trading coffee, wheat and the precious metals, but they are also trading heavily in stock index futures, interest rate futures and currencies. In other words, they are trading in many of the same things you would probably like to but cannot, because you either lack the required amounts of money to get started or do not fully understand the mechanics of the process.

Making profits in futures has always taken professional money management, proper capitalization and effective risk control. These relatively new funds have provided these factors for the smaller, more conservative investor.

To be sure, we are still not talking about an investment that ranks with government treasuries. But as an adjunct to an aggressive stock fund, commodities have their place.

We have already discussed the minimum amount you will need to get into the funds, and you generally will have to be able to show that your net worth is more than $75,000, excluding home and cars, or that your net worth is more than $30,000, with an income of more than $30,000 a year.

Most of the funds will charge a commission when you buy in and have ongoing fees for management as well. The fund managers usually are paid incentive fees, which are the nicest fees to have to pay, because they are keyed to the performance of the fund. There is usually no charge when you want to exit the program.

The liquidity of these funds is pretty good. Normally, you will have to stay in for at least several months, then you can come out, usually without a charge. However, you should plan to let these dollars work for at least a year or two.

Many of the programs offer several funds with varying degrees of risk. So you can spread your dollars out by going into a couple of funds or change your level of leverage as your personal finances change.

OBSTACLES TO OVERCOME
IN FUTURES TRADING

Even if you understand that trading in commodities has its economic advantages, if you are like most people, you still are reluctant to call a broker and initiate a trade.

And no wonder. The business is complex and quite different from other investing programs you may have undertaken.

Price movements in futures contracts are controlled by irrational factors such as weather and politics. There are no earnings reports to follow as you might use in picking stocks.

But, if you can afford to expose some of your investment dollars, you can diversify and potentially enjoy some aggressive capital growth through trading in futures contracts.

Let us examine why you hear so many horror stories from individuals who have traded commodities in the past.

Invariably, the most common problem traders experience is lack of sufficient capital to stay around long enough to pick up a trend.

Individual investors so often go into the market fully leveraged and when a correction takes place, instead of being able to come up with a little more money to ride the correction out, they are forced to liquidate their position and retreat to the back row of onlookers. Not unlike the typical scene around a blackjack table at Las Vegas.

Also, if an investor is under capitalized, he or she cannot diversify into several commodities. Their risk is maximized.

Then there is the emotion factor.

How many times have we known investors, who after getting beaten black and blue by their stocks going in the wrong direction, keep pouring good money into the stocks because they feel they cannot stop until they get even or that the stock owes them a good showing.

The fact is, most profits in commodities are not being made by the individual investor. Today, the full-time professional commodity trading adviser, using computer-assisted techniques, has enjoyed quite remarkable success.

Many of the advisers have been able to average returns after fees but before taxes — of about 30 to 45 percent over a period of a dozen years. Remember, that is an average.

The aggressiveness of commodity trading comes as a result of putting down only 10 percent of the value of the underlining contract value. Therefore, a very slight move will result in very large profits within hours or days.

There is another big difference between the futures market and the stock market when it comes to trading on margin. The stock market uses an initial requirement of 50 percent of the value of your purchase, and you pay interest to the brokerage firm for the balance of the funds needed to pay for the trade.

In commodity trading, the five to 10 percent that is invested is deposited as a sort of good faith deposit upon entering the market with your trade. You are not charged any interest on the remaining 90 to 95 percent. It is because of this high degree of leverage that a slight change in price say as little as 10 percent, can result in a 100-percent profit.

This leverage could work the other way as well. In this case you could be asked to put up additional money or have your position liquidated.

CHAPTER 31
CONVERTIBLES

CONVERTIBLES FOR INCOME AND GROWTH

Whenever the stock market goes into a prolonged period of stagnation, many investors grow weary of waiting for the next move up.

They have to weigh the loss on their invested dollars as they sit in growth stocks with little or no dividends, month after month. Money market funds or government funds start to look better all the time.

Now, it is difficult to say what investors should be doing without knowing them personally or their finances in great detail, but if you see yourself in this position sometimes, there are a number of strategies you might consider.

You could turn to option writing. You buy the stock and sell someone else an option to buy it from you at a slightly higher price. If the market moves up, you will get to share in some of the gain on your stock, and coupled with the premium you took in when you sold the option, you will have a very nice return for your efforts.

Something else you could do is just purchase stocks with a larger dividend, such as utility stocks, and figure you will give up going all for growth and settle for a nice dividend and still some expectation of price movement should the market surge ahead.

A less common method is to buy a convertible security, if there is one, in the company you are interested in owning.

For example, let us say you believe the stock market will be moving much higher over the next year and you want to share in that movement. You believe that XYZ selling around $125 is a quality stock that will move in this next push of the market. The stock has already traded at a little more than $138 this year, and many brokerage firms rate it a buy at today's price.

XYZ pays a small dividend, so at today's price, the yield on your investment while you wait for the stock price to move up is about 3 1/2 percent.

When you consider these same dollars could be earning more than twice that amount in a money market fund, you can better see the cost of your investment. If you do not need income, you can afford to wait months for the price movement you predict. However, if you need income as well as growth, you may be hurting yourself unless the stock moves quickly.

You could consider buying the XYZ convertible bond instead of the common stock. In our example, this bond has a coupon of 7 7/8 percent and gives you the right to convert your bond to shares of common stock in the same company any time you want, between now and when the bond matures.

Think about it. Because the bond has a fixed-rate coupon, you know you will at least always receive a decent level of income.

You also have the power to convert this bond into shares of the common. Because the bond has this flexibility, it trades very much in line with what the common stock is doing. So, the bond will move up, if and when, the common finally makes its move.

There is no question, it is a compromising position. You get some income and some prospect of growth. You can do this with convertible bonds or convertible preferred stock. Keep in mind that you are still tied basically to the strength of the underlying company so stay with companies you like very much.

If you do not feel you can do a good job of selecting quality firms or do not have much money to invest and like the idea but want more safety and someone else to do all the work for you, you should look into investing in a convertible mutual fund. Of course, read the prospectus first.

CHAPTER 32
NEW PRODUCTS

"GUARANTEED WAY" TO BE IN THE STOCK MARKET

For investors getting the itch to get back into the stock market but still suffering from October '87's crash, Wall Street has an idea to help you get over your jitters.

They are going to give you a guarantee.

And this is no idle guarantee. It is backed by the U. S. Government. Now, it is not a guarantee that you will make a profit, but the next best thing. They have guaranteed your original investment.

What they have done is created a package that combines a top-performing common stock fund with zero-coupon treasuries.

The dollars channeled into the growth fund give you the opportunity for appreciation. Enough dollars are allocated to the zero-coupon treasuries to ensure your original investment will be there after a period of years. It can vary, but right now eight to 10 years would be pretty typical.

The reason they can be so sure that they will be able to at least return your investment at the stated maturity date is that zero-coupon certificates, in this case treasuries, are securities that are purchased at a fraction of what they will be worth at maturity. For example, an investor can buy a zero-coupon treasury today for less than $400 and know if they hold it for 10 years, it will be worth exactly $1,000.

A few years ago when zeros were at double-digit yields, a lot of people with young children purchased them to pay for future college tuition. But today with yields considerably less, there is a greater necessity to have some growth from equities to meet future obligations.

This is why this investment idea, combining the safe predictable zero treasuries with the unpredictable common stock fund, would seem interesting to a lot of people. It certainly would lend itself to funding a retirement plan.

You can invest in multiples of $1,000. As with all unit trusts, you will usually pay a commission when purchasing the unit trusts but pay nothing to sell it if you should want to get out before the planned termination date.

Investors should keep in mind the guarantee to return your original investment is at maturity of the unit trusts only. Between now and then, the value of your investment will depend mainly on how well the dollars in the common stock portfolio do.

Of course, if the common stock portfolio does really well, you probably will have wished you had simply put all your dollars there and not gone into the special trust where part of your dollars went into zero-coupon treasuries offering a safe but lesser return.

And let us face it. If the stock fund does nothing and all you get back at the end of eight or 10 years is your original investment, you have still lost the potential return your money would have earned somewhere else during that time. But then again, you would not have had the opportunity to make potentially bigger gains that this unit trust offers.

Some experienced investors may say, "Hey, I can do that myself. I can put some of my money into zero-coupon treasuries and some into a good portfolio of stocks." And you certainly can. But packaged investments like this give you convenience and the advantage of working with millions of dollars even though you might just be investing a few thousand.

CHAPTER 33
DEFERRED ANNUITIES

DEFERRED ANNUITIES GIVE BETTER RETURN THAN CDs

In the weeks and months to come, you are going to see more and more ads talking about the advantages of deferred annuities over certificates of deposit.

And why not?

While both annuities and CDs are recognized as safe investments offering comparable yields on your money, the brokerage industry and insurance agents believe they have a superior product in annuities that was made even more advantageous following the passage of the new Medicare Catastrophic Act.

Here is why.

Depending on your age and circumstances, there could now be three major tax advantages deferred annuities have over CDs.

The first is the obvious one. All interest earned in an annuity escapes taxation until you elect to withdraw your interest. This means that if you deferred taking the interest for a couple of years and let it compound and then took it all out and paid taxes on the lump sum, you would be further ahead than your neighbor who annually took out his or her interest and paid taxes.

But you gain two other advantages by deferring taxes on your interest earned.

If you are receiving social security, you know by now you can be taxed on part of it, depending on how much income you show on your tax return. So it stands to reason, if you can avoid showing interest earned on a large sum of money, you have a better chance of staying below the threshold where the taxes start. The deferred annuity does not require you to show income earned until you take it out, whereas the CD produces interest to report as income, whether you elect to receive it or not.

And now we have another — the new Medicare Catastrophic Tax.

If you qualify for Medicare, whether you are on it or not, the tax starting in 1989 will cost you $22.50 for every $150 of tax you owe on your 1040 form, up to a cap of $800 for individuals and $1,600 for those filing a joint return. And over the next four years, the amounts will continually increase.

Again, because this new tax is a surtax, meaning it is an added tax on taxes you pay, you have another reason for wanting to keep your reportable income to a minimum. The deferred annuity can help you do that without giving up anything.

In the past, some viewed the annuity as being less liquid than the CD. But this is no longer the case. In fact, you could argue annuities are more liquid.

At the short end, there are one-year CDs and one-year annuities, each with no cost to go in and no cost to come out at the end of the year. However, if you try to come out of a CD early, the bank will normally charge you several months' interest even if you only purchased the CD a couple of days ago. Not so with annuities. At no time, even if you come out early, will you lose any of your principal.

If you go into a longer term CD for a higher yield, and you decide to go for another length of time when it matures, you start all over again with another penalty period. Not so with the deferred annuity. When its penalty period is up, you can simply go another year at a time.

DEFERRED ANNUITIES FOR SAFE MONEY STORAGE

You know how it goes. You hesitate to throw an old sweater or suit away, because it might just come in handy sometime. So you keep it in your closet, jamming up all the other clothes you use.

It is difficult to get rid of something we have enjoyed. Maybe you can try what I do sometimes. I say to myself, if I have not needed it for the past two years, then, like it or not, out it goes. Having the rule helps me remove the emotion from the decision process and forces me to do something I should have done much earlier.

And in going over many portfolios, I find it is very common for people to keep too much cash in a liquid money market fund.

If I ask these people why they do not have more of these dollars working in a tax-free bond or other investment, they will say they might need the cash someday and do not want to lock up the money.

I think there is another reason as well. And that is, many people equate having dollars in a money market fund with safety.

But keeping excess dollars in a money market fund could be costing you quite a bit, because you are robbing yourself of higher yields and safety that are available to you elsewhere.

For example, while money market funds are paying an attractive yield right now, by the time you subtract what you will pay in taxes, you are earning very little.

If you can bring yourself to doing it, you might consider putting money into a deferred annuity.

Deferred annuities pay about one percent more than money market funds. If you think interest rates are going to go back up soon, you can lock this rate up for one year and get a new rate of interest next year.

If you believe that rates are going to stay down at this level for years to come, or perhaps go even lower, you can lock up the rate for five years.

Either way, the interest earned will stay in and earn interest on itself. And because you have a deferred annuity, your earnings will not be taxed. This way the money that would have gone to taxes can earn interest for you as well.

This is why money grows so much faster in a deferred annuity, compared with a money market fund, government mutual fund or bank certificate of deposit.

Granted, you will pay taxes at some later date when you start pulling money out of your annuity. But no matter how you analyze it, you will be dollars ahead if you can save your extra cash in an annuity rather than a money market fund.

But what if you like using the interest your money is earning each year for paying bills?

Select a deferred annuity that gives you the option of withdrawing what your money earns each year. Some let you take the earnings out several times throughout the year while others only allow once-a-year withdrawals.

You should also try to select an annuity that allows you to take out interest earned from past years that you let accumulate. The added flexibility is nice.

Many tax changes have affected the flexibility of deferred annuities over the past decade. One of the last changes specifies that unless you are at least 59 1/2 years old, if you withdraw interest from your annuity, you will be subject to a 10-percent penalty. In all cases, the interest you withdraw is taxed as income.

NEW CD-ANNUITY HAS IT ALL

If you are looking to put some money in a place that will be safe but still pay a decent return, it is time you met the new CD-style annuity.

This innovative investment can be described as being more powerful than a regular certificate of deposit, because your earnings are all tax deferred and more liquid than a regular annuity. Also, you can take all your money out annually without any surrender charges.

The advantages of such an investment have apparently not been lost on Americans looking to find ways to save for retirement, as well as those who have already retired and want to be extra careful with their nest egg. Two or three other companies have already come out with similar plans.

The investment is actually a deferred annuity, meaning the dollars invested are safe. It also means all of the interest earned is exempt from income taxes until you start withdrawing the money. Currently, plans are paying about 8 percent to 8.5 percent. At the end of each year, a new interest rate is announced.

But here is its unique feature:

Once a year, at the time the company announces the coming interest rate for your plan, you have the right to take out all of your original principal, plus accumulated interest, without surrender charges.

If, on the other hand, you decide the interest rate declared for the coming year is again the best you could get for such a safe investment, you simply stay in for another year.

You also have the option of taking out just some of your money during the two months immediately following your anniversary renewal date.

Only if you decide to come out of the plan at some other time during the year will you be subject to a surrender charge. This is similar to breaking a certificate of deposit early. You are subject to a surrender penalty.

Setting an interest rate each year is an advantage. If these are to be your really safe dollars, you do not want to be trying to outguess the interest rate markets; you just want to know your dollars are earning a competitive rate of return. In this case, you have the added feature of not having those earnings taxed until you decide to take out the money.

To remind you just how significant tax deferral is when you are trying to save, consider this example.

These CD-type annuities are currently paying about 8.5- to 9-percent interest. So let us say you put $50,000 in a regular certificate and earned 8.5 percent. You are in a 28-percent tax bracket. After 10 years, you would have about $90,000.

But if you were getting the 8.5 percent in a deferred savings plan, it would be worth close to $115,000. Granted, you still have to pay taxes on the accumulated earnings, but you would do this only on how much you actually withdraw. The rest of your money continues to earn interest.

As good as this idea might be for so many people looking for a safe way to save and get ahead, there is an

218 YOUR INVESTMENT CHOICES

age factor to consider. No, not how old you must be to get in (typically, you can be 80 to 85 years old), but the age you are when you make withdrawals.

If you are under 59 1/2 years old, or think you will be using your earnings before then, think twice before going into the CD-style annuity. Current tax law requires a penalty of 10 percent to be applied to interest withdrawals from an annuity for owners of the contract under 59 1/2 years.

But this investment also can be a good alternative to funding your retirement plan. It will allow you to place money in a safe vehicle, usually with a higher interest rate than a one-year certificate of deposit and yet, requiring only a one-year holding period.

Annuities, unlike their late uptown relatives, the single premium life plans, have no health requirement to get into the investment.

SECTION FOUR: YOUR OWN PLAN

FREE OFFER

Author and Certified Financial Planner Richard DuPuis makes this free offer to you to help you and your family get better organized and perhaps save you tax dollars.

If you would like to have him review your estate plan and send you a 5-10 page report showing your current situation and how you might better arrange your affairs to pass your assets on to your loved ones with the least amount of costs and delay, simply fill in the forms **on the following pages** and send them, along with your check for $5, to cover handling, to Companion Books, Suite 160-27, 900 North Federal Highway, Boca Raton, Florida 33432. We will acknowledge receipt of your forms and forward them to Mr. DuPuis. This is a limited offer.

TEST YOUR MARKET SAVVY CONTEST

There is a famous saying that says, "As General Motors goes, so goes the country." Well, perhaps in the last number of years GM has had to share the spotlight with some other major companies. But in any event, the stock market has long been thought of as a precursor of things to come. So our contest [See the return card at the back of this book for details.] has to do with predicting where the Dow Jones Industrial Average is going. Good luck!

> GOT A QUESTION ABOUT FILLING OUT THE FORMS? CALL THIS HOTLINE NUMBER, 1-800- 962-5564.

PLANNING YOUR ESTATE
Richard DuPuis, CFP
Director of Financial Planning

I. PERSONAL INFORMATION

    A. Your Name _____

        Spouse's Name _____

        Address _____

        Phone No. _____

    B. Your Marital Status: _____

            1 — Married Male   3 — Single Male
            2 — Married Female   4 — Single Female

    C. Your Birthday: _____

        Spouses' Birthdate: _____

    D. State of Residence: _____

II. INVESTMENT ASSETS

    Fill in the current value of the investment asset, how it is held, who the owner of the asset is, and the heir. Extra spaces have been provided for those assets not listed or separately held/owned assets of the same type.

HELD: 1 — Directly, 2 — Pension, 3 — Profit-Sharing, 4 — Keogh,
       5 — IRA, 6 — 401K, 7 — Other
OWNER: 1 — You, 2 — Spouse, 3 — Joint, 4 — Community Property
HEIR: 1 — Surviving Spouse, 2 — Charity, 3 — Other

TYPE	CURRENT VALUE	HELD	OWNER	HEIR
Liquid Assets	$ _____	_____	_____	_____
Municipal Bonds	$ _____	_____	_____	_____
Taxable Bonds	$ _____	_____	_____	_____
Common Stocks	$ _____	_____	_____	_____
Partnerships	$ _____	_____	_____	_____
Retirement Accts	$ _____	_____	_____	_____
_____	$ _____	_____	_____	_____
_____	$ _____	_____	_____	_____
_____	$ _____	_____	_____	_____
_____	$ _____	_____	_____	_____
_____	$ _____	_____	_____	_____

III. DEBTS

All debts, except business debts, should be listed here, including home mortgages and other consumer debt (credit cards, car loans, etc.). List the nature of the debt, current loan amount and the purpose and responsibility.

PURPOSE: 1 — Personal, 2 — Business, 3 — Investment,
    4 — Home Mortgage
RESPONSIBILITY: 1 — You, 2 — Spouse, 3 — Joint,
    4 — Community Property

NAME OF DEBT	AMOUNT	PURPOSE	RESPONSIBILITY
1. _____	$ _____	_____	_____
2. _____	$ _____	_____	_____
3. _____	$ _____	_____	_____
4. _____	$ _____	_____	_____
5. _____	$ _____	_____	_____

IV. PERSONAL ASSETS

List here the current value of all personal assets (homes, boats, cars, jewelry, personal assets, etc.) as well as the owner and heir of each asset:

OWNER: 1 — You 2 — Spouse, 3 — Joint, 4 — Community Property
HEIR: 1 — Spouse, 2 — Charity, 3 — Other

	VALUE	OWNER	HEIR
Residence 1	$ _____	_____	_____
Residence 2	$ _____	_____	_____
Boat	$ _____	_____	_____
Vehicle 1	$ _____	_____	_____
Vehicle 2	$ _____	_____	_____
Jewelry	$ _____	_____	_____
_____	$ _____	_____	_____
_____	$ _____	_____	_____
_____	$ _____	_____	_____
_____	$ _____	_____	_____
_____	$ _____	_____	_____

V. REAL ESTATE AND BUSINESS INTERESTS

List any real estate, operating partnerships and proprietorships which are *directly owned* (apartment and/or commercial buildings or other rental property) *and managed by you.*

HELD: 1 — Directly-Owned, 2 — Pension, 3 — Profit Sharing,
    4 — Keogh, 5 — IRA, 6 — 401K, 7 — Other
OWNER: 1 — You, 2 — Spouse, 3 — Joint, 4 — Community Property
HEIR: 1 — Spouse, 2 — Charity, 3 — Other

	CURRENT VALUE	HELD	OWNER	HEIR
Real Estate	$ _____	_____	_____	_____
Real Estate	$ _____	_____	_____	_____
_____	$ _____	_____	_____	_____
_____	$ _____	_____	_____	_____
_____	$ _____	_____	_____	_____
_____	$ _____	_____	_____	_____
_____	$ _____	_____	_____	_____
_____	$ _____	_____	_____	_____

REAL ESTATE AND BUSINESS DEBTS

List all debt related to above real estate and business interest.

PURPOSE: 1 — Personal, 2 — Business, 3 — Investment
RESPONSIBILITY: 1 — You, 2 — Spouse, 3 — Joint,
    4 — Community Property

NAME OF DEBT	AMOUNT	PURPOSE	RESPONSIBILITY
1. _____	$ _____	_____	_____
2. _____	$ _____	_____	_____
3. _____	$ _____	_____	_____

VI. INSURANCE

List all life insurance policies, including the face amount, the insured party, owner, beneficiary, and any policy loans outstanding.

INSURED: 1 — You, 2 — Spouse, 3 — Children, 4 — Other
OWNER: 1 — You, 2 — Spouse, 3 — Trust, 4 — Estate
    5 — Community Property, 6 — Other
BENEFICIARY: 1 — Surviving Spouse, 2 — Trust, 3 — Children,
    4 — Other

FACE AMOUNT	INSURED	OWNER	BENEFI-CIARY	POLICY LOANS
$ _____	_____	_____	_____	_____
$ _____	_____	_____	_____	_____
$ _____	_____	_____	_____	_____
$ _____	_____	_____	_____	_____

VII. ATTITUDES AND OBJECTIVES

A. Check the statement that best describes your current will:

	You	Spouse
1. No will	_____	_____
2. A handwritten will	_____	_____
3. A will with no trusts	_____	_____
4. A will with (a) testamentary trust(s)	_____	_____
5. A will combined with a revocable living trust	_____	_____

IF YOU DO NOT HAVE A WILL, SKIP TO QUESTION G

B. In what year was your will last revised or written? _____

C. In what year was your last change in marital status? _____

D. In what year was your last move from another state? _____

E. Does your will do the following (Y/N):

    1. Name a personal representative or executor? _____

    2. Name a successor executor? _____

    3. Name a presumed survivor in the event of simultaneous death? _____

    4. Provide for a contingent trust? _____

    5. Provide for a trustee for the contingent trust? _____

    6. Name a guardian for your children? _____

F. Are you currently using any of the following trust estate planning ideas (Y/N):

    1. Surviving Spouse (Marital Trust)? _____

    2. Exemption (unified credit) Trust? _____

    3. Qualified terminable interest property trust (Q-TIP)? _____

    4. Holding a level of assets in the estate of the first to die that exceeds the amount exempted by the unified credit? _____

    5. Insurance Trust? _____

G. Check the statement that best describes your feelings about providing investment management and advice for your survivors in the event of your death:

    1. My survivors have the experience and capacity to manage without outside help. _____

    2. I would like to make arrangements now that will insure my survivors are provided with assistance in financial decisions. _____

H. Check which one of the following statements best describes your feelings about keeping your financial affairs private:

    1. I am not willing to reorganize my financial affairs just to keep them private. _____

    2. Privacy is very important. _____

Mail To:
Richard DuPuis, CFP
Director of Financial Planning
c/o Companion Books
900 North Federal Highway
Suite 160-27
Boca Raton, FL 33432